Get it
Right

Get it
Right

Published in 2003 by Farming Books and Videos Ltd.

ISBN 09542555-69

A catalogue record for this book is available from the British Library.

Published by
Farming Books and Videos Ltd.
PO Box 536
Preston
PR2 9ZY
United Kingdom
www.farmingbooksandvideos.com

Book designed and set by
Surface
T. 01702 232058

Printed by
Unwin Brothers of Woking

Contents

Acknowledgments

Without friends books are so much harder to write, for they are the silent ones, the ones that support, advise, assist, encourage and motivate but are seldom mentioned. They are the ones who are there to discuss things with and from whom we often get inspiration.

But in this instance I have not only been fortunate in having friends that did all of these things but in also having some that played an active part in contributing to this book.

Friends such as Paula Wright, who generously took many of the splendid photographs as well as designing the footwork patterns throughout this book and whose support and encouragement in general has been unrelenting. She is a very talented lady who I owe a huge thank you to.

To Eleanor Gordon Macdonald for the front cover photograph I also owe the same thanks.

To Jenni Watson for the much appreciated Foreword.

To my son Oliver for taking other photographs which had been overlooked. Thanks Ollie

And lastly, but by no means least, thanks to another very special girl and her kennel mates past and present who, without their help over the years, this book could not have been written and a much less understanding a person I would have been.

Poppi
Taminacky Twinkling Gem

Jaff
Dunnslayne All Gold at Borderstorm

Merlin
Dawnview Movement

Boots
Bootiful Boy

Merlin's sons Spell & Drift
Spell of Heronsmead + Sorcerer of Heronsmead

'Those that are here are so precious and keep dark clouds at bay
Those that are gone were beacons that first showed me the way'

Foreword by Jenni Watson

I cannot think of any living person who is more of a Border Collie enthusiast than Roy Goutté. I first met Roy in the mid 1980s when he was heavily into Competitive Obedience and enjoying a very successful time competing with his beautiful tri-coloured Border Collie, Merlin, and a couple of Merlin's offspring. When he moved to Cornwall some years ago he embarked on a unique career in providing a pedigree and breeding service to the Border Collie fraternity. The results of Roy's findings have served as a bible to Border Collie breeders and lovers the world over. Roy has studied and catalogued almost every Border Collie pedigree in the land. Today, any person considering breeding from their stock, or buying in a puppy from any working lines, can contact Roy who will willingly give advice regarding 'what to use' or 'what to buy'. Backing this up has been a series of books written by Roy relating to Border Collie ancestry. The 'Principal Lines' supplies the reader with all the knowledge required to gain an impression of the history of breeding lines of Border Collies in all disciplines that it takes part in.

Never a man to sit still and believing that if you haven't tried it, don't knock it, Roy has competed in Sheepdog Trialling for some years now and has been deeply involved in re-introducing the bloodlines of the trialling bred Border Collie back into Obedience and to its founding roots. As the Border Collie is such a versatile dog it will respond willingly to many areas of work and sport if placed in the right hands and none better than Roy's who has personal and successful experience of training the working Border Collie from a farming background.

So now Roy has returned to his own roots for his latest book, obedience training. He would be the first to appreciate that there are many varied methods of training an Obedience bred dog, but it is his thoughts and methods, based on his own practical experiences, that the reader will enjoy learning about in this book.

Jenni Watson
Principal, Academy of Dog Training and Behaviourists (ADTB).

Jenni Watson has owned and trained two Obedience Champions, one Breed Champion and qualified a third dog at Crufts in Obedience and Breed. Her dogs have won 33 Obedience Championship Certificates and she has featured in and produced 3 videos covering pet and competitive obedience training. At Crufts 2003 she had the distinction of judging the Junior Kennel Club Test of Obedience Competitions.

Preface

There is nothing quite like owning an obedient dog. It doesn't matter whether that dog is a family pet or a working dog actively taking part in one of the many varying disciplines that dogs can participate in, for a well behaved dog is a joy to own.

What does matter, however, is that you have taken the time to train your dog to a standard which confidently enables him to take part in Obedience Competitions. This shows that you have acted responsibly towards your dog and are allowing him to have a full and beneficial life in the home and in the community.

I owned my first dogs, both rescues, at seventeen years of age. However there had been dogs in the family since my early childhood. My father had once owned a German Shepherd Dog during the Second World War while living in Jersey. Although the dog's name escapes me, he did not escape the attention of the Germans who occupied the islands at the time. Father had been caught riding his bike after curfew and a German officer had brought him home. On entering the house the dog immediately ran up the stairs and brought my father's slippers down to him. The German officer, being impressed by the dog's intelligence, took an instant like to him and confiscated him. The family never saw him again!

He was followed some years later by Pluto, a Cocker Spaniel with the most perfect of temperaments and brain to suit. My boyhood years were spent in his company and I suppose must in parts be responsible for my love of working dogs. I felt he was really special and two memories of him stand out more than any other.

We lived in the village of Gorey and during the summer months we always picnicked on the local Grouville Bay beach on a Sunday. This particular Sunday after returning home, my mother discovered that we had left a 'bread and butter' plate on the beach. I can remember my father saying that Pluto would go and fetch it. He then put him out of the kitchen door telling him to go and find it.

Being just a child I never thought any more about it until the next morning when my mother commented that Pluto had not come back. Well my father had hardly gone out of the door to look for him when both he and the dog returned, together with the plate!

It transpired that Pluto had made his way to the beach the previous evening only to find the tide had covered the area where we had picnicked, so he had settled down there for the night waiting for the tide to recede. This was confirmed by a golfing pal who had actually seen Pluto digging in the sand in the early hours just after sunrise and by another person who had seen him on the beach late in the evening while taking his own dog out for a walk. The golfing friend actually witnessed Pluto discover the plate and run off with it in his mouth where at some stage he must have met up with my father who had just gone out to look for him.

On the other occasion it nearly cost Pluto his life. There were some 'travellers' camping on our village green and I can well remember mother warning my brother and I to keep well clear of them! One night we were all awoken by the terrible sound of breaking glass followed by Pluto crying in pain. A traveller had tried to break into our house and was actually in our rear porch where he had disturbed Pluto who always slept under the kitchen table. Not being able to get to the intruder through the door itself he had hurled himself through the large kitchen widow and severely lacerated himself on the glass in the process. My father came downstairs to find the traveller still in the porch, too terrified to come out, with Pluto outside the porch door in the most distressed of conditions with deep wounds to his entire body. It was only some years later, when I understood more, that my father told me that he didn't know what happened to the intruder as he had been so concerned about getting the dog to the vet as quickly as possible that he let him escape.

But time moves on and I left Jersey at the age of sixteen. I may have left the island, but I didn't leave my love of working dogs behind for a new dog had entered my life, the Border Collie.

In 1968 and now living and working in Southampton, I went on holiday with my parents. We were touring around the south of England and started in the Salisbury area where we saw a sheepdog trial advertised. I had never been to a trial before. I didn't even know they existed but nevertheless popped in to have a look. It was to change my life!

It was a very hot day and whilst enjoying what I was seeing it meant very little to me as I did not understand quite what was happening other than what was obvious and I certainly couldn't make head or tail of the marking system. I was fascinated by the intense concentration shown by most of the dogs when confronted with their sheep. Although always having dogs in the family I had only ever encountered such focus once before in a dog and that was with Pluto.

It was one particular dog however that captured my imagination and solely because of the extraordinary way that he went about his work. He caused a catalyst and it is this catalyst that has been responsible for me religiously delving into the bloodlines of the Border Collie ever since to try to discover what makes them tick.

I remember that magic day as if it were yesterday. I had watched many dogs run but was beginning to get a little bored. What with every dog appearing to be the equal of each other and the oppressive heat bearing down on competitor, dog and spectator alike, I thought of retiring to the refreshment tent. The thought didn't last long, however, for suddenly people who had been aimlessly wandering about began to move closer to the temporary fence that had been erected for the trial. Something was afoot!

A new dog and handler had arrived at the post and from the moment they set foot into the arena the crowd became restless and were talking excitedly. What was going on I wondered?

The most handsome of Collies was parading by his handler's side, but it wasn't his handler he was interested in - just those specks of white in the distance! He was bristling all over with excitement and on command, left his handler's side like a rocket to begin his outrun. His outrun was to the right and he flashed passed me like there was no tomorrow, clinging like glue to the temporary fence that had been erected. He got well behind his sheep - too far it seemed to my inexperienced eyes - before turning. Then they were off!

I have of course been to many a trial since and have seen dogs take sheep around at breakneck speeds, but I don't think I have ever seen a dog take sheep around a course as quickly as he did, but under complete control! I was totally fascinated and in awe as he went about his work. He was on his feet throughout the entire run, never downing once, and it seemed over in no time.

Throughout all the other runs I had been aware of plenty of shouting and whistling by the handlers but in this instance I had heard very little. Was this my imagination or did the dog do it all by himself? Well of course he didn't but for me that was the magic of this dog for his approach to his work was so all consuming that he took my normal senses away. I became oblivious to all outside distractions, I had become like him. As he was totally committed to his craft, so I had become totally committed to him. To all intents and purposes, the dog and I had become one!

I have come to appreciate since, that for me, he was the ultimate exception - the one in a million - and I shall never forget him. He was Llyr Evans' Bosworth Coon.

That autumn, Coon became the International Supreme Champion.

From there on in I just had to have a Border Collie but as we were living in a flat at the time it was out of the question.

Then, in 1975, when my circumstances changed, I went to view a litter of pups born to a Border Collie bitch. The sire was of ill repute and an even more dubious parentage, but I liked what I saw and purchased a nearly pure black puppy. As it was only his two front paws that were white, I named him Boots.

Having a really excitable collie cross who would never settle unless he was doing something, I joined a Competitive Obedience training club in Twyford near Winchester to help settle him. Like many before and no doubt like many will in the future, I became hooked on the sport.

Boots was hard work as he had a pathological hatred of all other dogs. He was a nightmare to take into a stay ring for the moment the command 'Exercise finished' was uttered by the stay steward, he would dive into the nearest dog. However I trained him well and between us we won two Beginners, three Novices and two A classes before I retired him because I couldn't stand the pressure of having a dog that you had to watch like a hawk every moment another dog came anywhere near him. He was retired at just three years of age but lived until one week short of his nineteenth birthday.

It was then that Merlin came into my life. With a Kennel Club name of Dawnview Movement, he was everything I ever wanted and a real Border Collie.

He cut through the classes like a knife through butter and I thought I was in heaven. In the meantime he sired a litter of pups of which I kept two back, Spell and Drift. In no time at all Merlin had reached Class C and was on the threshold of qualifying for Championship C.

I entered an indoor show in Devon and was well in the lead losing just 1.5 points with just scent discrimination to go. With my heart racing I set Merlin up and sent him on his way to what I hoped was to be my dream day. He worked every cloth in a way that displayed what a good dog he was and came across 'it' at the conclusion of his search. Picking the cloth up cleanly he started to make his way back to me in a very positive manner. I can still remember thinking to myself how short the journey would be driving back home knowing that I had now reached 'Ticket'.

Merlin moved back across the ring and turned in to present the cloth to me, and dropped it at my feet! He had presented without it and sat there looking up at me with a cheesy grin on his face - while the cloth lay on the floor!!

What a journey that was home that evening. All Obedience folk will know that feeling but also know that it only lasts for a short while as there is always a show and another opportunity to recoup losses the following weekend.

And this is exactly what happened with Merlin and I. The following week he did win and then again the following weekend. My boy had made it!

It was then that my world fell apart.

We were now qualified to enter Championship C and so I entered him at Littlebourne Championship show. His brilliance shone through and at his first attempt he was leading the class with just stays to go. Sadly he was to fail them, not an uncommon thing for Merlin to do, but I was overjoyed that he competed well at the very highest level.

In his following show he led again until scent where he was then joined on equal marks by another dog due to a small error he made while working the scent pattern. But all chance of even having a run-off for first place was dashed when he again broke stays.

Then, on his third show when a handsome leader, he failed scent for the first time in ticket. It was entirely my fault as my nerves got the better of me and caused him to become uncertain and hurried so he brought back the decoy cloth that was lying next to the positive one.

This, as it turned out, was to be Merlin's last serious attempt at winning a ticket as he contracted toxoplasmosis by eating cats droppings out of a litter tray. It was to finish his career at only three years of age.

I took him to the vet the week after his scent failure because I noticed that he didn't seem to be extending himself in his training. The home side of his life was perfectly normal but his 'edge' had gone when being trained.

To make a long story a short one, the veterinary college at Bristol discovered he had toxoplasma and as at that time there was no cure, I was advised not to work him any more. I was told it would not shorten his life but as I had found out, he would not be able to extend himself in a working situation.

I decided to work him just one more time so entered the ticket class at Surrey Championship Show. Heelwork was the last test in the round so he had time to settle in. He put up a good performance in the other exercises and would have been lying well up with the leaders. Considering he had had no work to speak of for weeks I was well pleased. However, come the heelwork and the truth was revealed. Try as he did he could not keep up and to my dying day I will remember the words of a lady walking with a friend outside of the ring I was working in, when she turned to her friend and said "How did that awful dog ever get into ticket?"

For the first time in my life I walked straight out of a ring without thanking the judge or steward. I felt destroyed and drove straight home. Merlin never worked again but lived to the grand old age of eighteen before dying of a stroke.

I've had great pleasure in working two other dogs in ticket and two others in C only. My wife's dog, Fly (Wyvo's Copper Drummer) and Black & White Roy were both real tryers who could easily, with a bit more luck, have done so well. Fly won a reserve CC and I picked up a couple of Cs with him. With Roy I won my very first Open C at his and my first time of asking.

Jim (Pinglestone Jim) has given me enormous pleasure. A son of John Templeton's record breaking trialling dog Roy 114678 (ISDS) the triple Scottish National Champion and dual reserve International Supreme Champion, he cannot be faulted for his commitment even though he has health problems but still reached C only. He is a credit to his breeding.

Then along came my Jaff (Dunnslayne All Gold At Borderstorm). A natural worker and a successful combination of Obedience and Sheepdog Trialling lines, he encapsulated all that was good in working a happy dog in Obedience Competition. Again, with Jaff, I reached C only, but because an opportunity arose whereby we were able to purchase a property with land, I decided to withdraw from Obedience competition. I used the break to concentrate on learning to train a Border Collie for sheep work and to also expand my dog breeding programme that I had started some years earlier.

As my sheepdog training has gone so well and my breeding programme has become firmly established breeding the ISDS registered Border Collies, I have now re-commenced my Obedience training. I have taken on an Obedience bred three year old bitch called Poppi and plan to be competing again in 2003.

And if all of that wasn't enough, many in Obedience and Sheepdog Trialling will know of my books on the bloodlines of the Border Collie/Working Sheepdog in Obedience, Sheepdog Trialling and the Breed world. I also write a 'Bloodlines' series for Dog Training Weekly and International Sheepdog News and run a very successful Border Collie pedigree service. It doesn't take much working out that I lead a very busy and active life!

Roy Goutté
2003.

Introduction

Pre-Training

Welcome to GET IT RIGHT! This is a carefully structured dog training programme aimed at the competitive minded person who is already competing in, or would like to compete in, Open and Championship Obedience Competition. It also gives plenty of suggestions and useful tips for general obedience training.

Before we start I feel it appropriate to offer a brief note of explanation if not an apology. I am more than aware that I have referred throughout the book to the dog as a 'him'. I did attempt, in my submission manuscript, to use 'it' or even 'he/she.' I even experimented with alternate genders every other chapter. It all got confusing, complicated and got in the way of the text. In the end I settled for 'he' and hope that this does not offend.

In this programme I will suggest ways that you can improve your already gained knowledge by offering useful additional advice. Or, if you are a total beginner with enough determination, guide you on your way to owning a happy and well trained dog that will do you credit and could take you right through to the very top level of Obedience Competition.

One of the very first things you will get to realise about dog training, no matter what the discipline, is that all dogs, even those of the same breeding, are not the same and certainly don't respond in the same manner. Some are a dream and take to training most willingly, but many others are sheer hard work! To succeed you often have to be as determined as the most awkward dog is obstinate, but at the end of the day, if successful, the rewards are limitless.

Top Tips

■ Remember! Not all dogs are the same and certainly do not respond to training in the same way.

Poppi, daughter of the 1995 Crufts Obedience Championship winner, Dalemain Red Rascal.

Carol Clack's Dalemain Red Rascal, Crufts Obedience Championship Winner 1995.

Top Tips

■ Remember! Obedience is a team effort: You and your dog.

So, how do we go about all this and are there any secrets? Well, yes there are, but the secrets all lie with you. You can go on as many training courses as you choose and see experienced instructors handling their dogs in ways that you never thought possible before, but, at the end of the day, the training of your dog is up to you. You are the one that takes your dog home and are responsible for getting the best out of him. Listen and observe well and take the best of the advice that is going to suit your dog - not all will - and put it into practice. Couple this with sheer determination, patience by the bucketful, a whole heap of luck and you are on the way to cracking it. This is the only secret, hard, but rewarding work.

Now let's get down to the nitty-gritty and discuss how we are going to go about this. I will assume that you have already come into the ownership of a fully grown dog or puppy and that other than desire a well-controlled pet, you would also like to put on that extra bit of polish and train your four-legged friend for competitive Obedience Competition. By carefully following the advice given in this book I believe you will stand a much greater chance of achieving that aim than if you were to take a haphazard approach and teach the set exercises in a less organised and progressive manner.

Some say that success in Obedience can only come with the right dog and to a degree that has to be true. However you also have to be the right handler for that dog as Obedience is a team effort. So, if there really is a secret to dog training, then it is that you and your four-legged friend make the most of your training time together and Get It Right!

In this book I have featured Poppi, (Taminacky Twinkling Gem) a Working Sheepdog I have taken on. She is a daughter of the 1995 Crufts Obedience Championship winner, Obedience Champion Dalemain Red Rascal. Occasionally, for demonstration purposes, I also feature Holly, (Hawks Tor Festive Spring) a young daughter of Jaff, (Dunnslayne All Gold At Borderstorm).

Chapter 1

Where to train

I am a great believer in commencing training in total seclusion without any off-putting visible distractions or loud noises whatsoever. This is the time to be at one with your four-legged friend at this crucial stage. Many is the time I have looked back and wished I had realised this sooner!

Once the basics have been taught to a good standard, then, as confidence grows, normal distractions can be introduced slowly into the work. In every other aspect your dog will be joining in the hurly-burly of life so later on noises in general should not be a problem for him. A quiet local park, or well protected corner of a field is ideal, or if you have private access to a hall, even better for those wet days.

The most obvious place of course is a room in your own home and certainly this is ideal in the early days of puppy training. This is a good place to start, but do avoid distractions and movement, especially from children and other dogs or pets running around.

When to train and how often

Train when it is best for both of you is the easy answer. When your dog and you can be together without you worrying about doing other things or having other pressing commitments. Don't snatch the odd five minutes when training will be hurried, better use of that time would be spent in your armchair mulling over how you will go about training a particular exercise, or alternate ways if things don't go according to plan. Most of all, be patient and make training that special time when close bonding between handler and dog is at its peak.

How to train

Train very carefully and with great patience. It is not natural and most dogs take time to become accustomed to a strict training programme. Playing is very stimulating and they normally achieve this through their mother or other siblings early in their lives. Combine play with your training and you will have already discovered one of the shortcuts that can help lead to success.

Top Tips

- Remember! Begin all training in a quiet, secluded spot with no distractions.

- Remember! Training should be a special quality time.

A knotted sock or manufactured 'tuggie' make great play toys for dogs and are used for both stimulation and for those moments when things aren't going quite right. Food, titbits in particular, are another major stimulus and provide a useful short-cut. Again we will see how they can be used to encourage a dog to achieve drive and enthusiasm for his new type of work.

Most of all, your training must be consistent and based on well-proven methods. All techniques in use today are just extensions of previous methods that have been around for years in one form or another but have simply evolved into a more accepted way of doing things. Other than a decent footwork pattern which is comparatively modern, there is really nothing new on display, just variations on an old theme with maybe a bit more thought put into it. It is the consistency of your training that is important and knowing what methods are best suited to your dog and you as the handler. In other words, it is a team effort!

The age to start training

For a puppy it is as soon as you feel that he gains confidence and is capable of understanding just some simple basic commands. Don't leave it too late as you could have a battle on your hands. Catch them while they are naturally receptive to learning and willing for you to educate them. After all, we are now their adopted parents!

With an untrained older or rescued dog, you really are giving yourself a challenge, but it has been faced many times before with success and training should commence from the moment a bond begins to form between you, but don't push it!

What exercises do I start with?

The following chapter will discuss some elementary very easy and progressive training exercises to begin with. Some may seem out of order for the early ring work expected of your dog, but we are covering them in preparation of the more advanced work to follow at a later date. There are some exercises - or at least parts of some exercises - which are best introduced while a dog is still a pup. This is when he is much more receptive to certain aspects of his training. These will be explained as training progresses.

Top Tips

■ Remember! Discover a short cut by combining play with your training.

Pre-Training

There are certain pre-training 'exercises' you can carry out prior to the commencement of full-time training. If you are contemplating the use of titbits as a training aid there is a very useful tip well worth adopting which involves very little effort on the part of the handler.

If you have had the satisfaction of breeding your own pup then this can be put into practice from the very moment you begin weaning your litter. If you have bought in your pup or indeed have just taken on an older dog, this commences with his very first meal in his new home.

It is a simple matter of just making a 'shushing' sound about four times with your mouth as you place your dog's feed bowl on the ground at feeding times. This 'shushing' sound, which is quite a new sound to a pup, has the desired effect of gaining instant attention. Because of this they soon realise that it is always followed by food. A litter is fed about four times a day. A young pup is fed about three times a day. Within just twenty-four hours they have learnt to come to you at breakneck speed when they hear this sound. It never ceases to amaze me how quickly they pick this up. It is fun to see but should be taken very seriously nevertheless and under no circumstances should you use the sound without rewarding them with food or a titbit.

What you have achieved of course is the beginning of the Come when Called exercise, which in time will be honed to perfection prior to competing in the ring.

Other exercises that can be started very early with titbits are the Sendaway and Distant Control and these will be explained fully in their respective chapters.

You can also train your dog to sit at your left side. This is the accepted working side in the Obedience ring.

Top Tips

■ Remember! The 4 Ps of Training; Planning, Playing, Patience and Praise.

17

First Things First

First though, you must spend considerable time with your dog forming a bond. Having a puppy is one thing, but if you have been compassionate enough to have rescued a dog, then the chances are that the dog you have taken on board is either nervous of you and strangers or possibly aggressive to other dogs. Whatever the situation he is going to require your undivided attention and love during a settling in period. This can take any amount of time depending very much on the dog's past experiences. But as a rule of thumb, we would generally be looking at about four to eight weeks of happy walks combined with reassuring hugs and games to gain a dogs confidence. During this quality time you can teach your dog the basic sit at your left-hand sit, (the working side) and also just general sitting and lying down.

It is also worth remembering that many a rescued or re-homed collie comes from farms and smallholdings well away from public access or gaze and many of the dogs will be wary of strangers. These dogs need to be given plenty of time to settle into a new environment. This gives you time to get them accustomed to your lifestyle.

Many people will put a newly acquired dog into a situation that he is obviously unhappy with taking the view that he is just going to have to get on with it. But if you are to get the best out of your dog then you must be sensible and take things slowly and stay well within his capabilities.

I once had a working collie brought to me for assessment by a Border Collie Rescue Society. He was extremely wary of strangers and would back away and growl when anyone approached him. Fortunately I had a well-known supermarket some five miles away from where I lived so was able to just walk the dog around the car parking area thus allowing him to get the feel of life outside the farm. We graduated slowly to a bench seat adjacent to the main door and would just sit there watching the world and the customers go by. Within a few days the aggression and apprehension began to disappear to be replaced by inquisitiveness towards the shopping trolleys and their contents and the joy of being offered sweets and reassuring pats by the children as they left the store with their parents. Eventually the dog was re-homed into an Obedience and Agility home where he enjoyed many years of competition and companionship.

Top Tips

■ Remember! Always take things slowly and stay within your dog's level of ability.

Chapter 2

The first three steps

When I commence training I have three initial aims:-

- To get my dogs to Come When Called.
- To perform an Instant Down
- To begin the Sendaway.

The Come When Called, coupled with its associated hand signal, is going to become as much a part of an Obedience dog's life as anything else that he will encounter. When you are carrying out a Pre-Beginner, Beginner, Novice or 'A' Recall it will come into play in one form or another, with or without a voice command. It also comes into play in the Retrieve in all classes, the Recall from the Sendaway area in both 'B' and 'C' and in all Scent tests. In short, it is part of nearly all major exercises whenever a dog has to return to you.

The **Instant Down**, Obedience apart, is a life-saver. I teach my dogs this at the very earliest opportunity, without them even realising it. At the same time I teach the **Come When Called**. Obedience wise, the Instant Down exercise is for use in the Sendaway exercise and to a limited degree in the Down Stay. The two however must not be confused!

I mentioned earlier that the use of titbits or a play toy would be of great benefit for the dog that reacts to either, not all do of course. The **Come When Called** is the perfect exercise to waken or gain their interest. In our very first exercise I shall be using both.

We start by getting the dog to **Come When Called**. At the same time we create an obstacle in his path that will encourage him to move into an **Instant Down** position momentarily, without any fear or force from you.

The Instant Down

What I am about to explain is so easy to teach that absolutely anyone can do it providing they are prepared to go to the trouble of setting things up. You may want to enlist the help of a member of the family or a friend to help you hold your dog. But it can be just as easily taught by you with just your trusted knotted sock and titbits as a reward.

The bottom rail of the gate is raised above the ground with sufficient gap under to allow your dog to crawl under it.

Your dog will realise that he has to crawl under the gate to reach you.

At my home in Cornwall I have a five-acre field which I exercise and train my sheepdogs in. I have a small flock of Scottish Blackface sheep for training purposes and various holding pens that I move them into when I need to inspect them. All of the pens have gates on them, and it is one such pen, and in particular the gate, that I teach my dogs the Instant Down under. I could have just as easily taught them this under a garden gate, or any such situation that would offer me the same facility. This is a gate that has a gap for the dog to crawl under!

The bottom rail of the gate is raised above the ground with sufficient gap beneath to allow your dog to crawl under whilst on the move without stopping until told to do so.

To begin this exercise leave your dog in a stand, sit, or down position roughly five metres behind the open gate. Position yourself on the opposite side of the gate at a comfortable distance while holding a toy, knotted sock or titbit.

It doesn't matter what position your dog is in as long as he is not worried or phased in any way. If your dog is not happy to wait while you make your way to the other side of the entrance you will need to get a friend to hold him for a few seconds.

When ready make the shushing noise with your mouth to gain his attention. Call your dog using the command Come. The moment he reaches you reward him with a titbit and a massive game of tug with its knotted sock or play toy. Repeat this three to four times more.

You will now repeat the exercise again. This time close the gate and kneel down a metre or two behind it on the opposite side to the dog with a titbit or play toy in your hand.

Make the shushing noise as before. When your dog begins to run to the now closed gate show him the titbit low down on the ground and underneath the gate. As he works out that he has to crawl on his belly under the gate to get his reward move your hand back slowly to entice him right through. On completion give him the titbit and lavish great praise on the dog ending with a game.

Your dog won't have realised it of course but he has completed his first Instant Down - albeit on the move!

As your dog goes under the gate check him by gently holding him down.

Repeat this about half a dozen times to gain complete confidence before moving to the next stage which is to keep your dog in the down position until released on command.

What you have done is to allow your dog to willingly get into a down position without touching or commanding him. He performed the action naturally. You are now going to instill the command to that action. This will remain with him for the rest of his life!

Leave your dog again in the sit, stand or down position and crouch down immediately behind the far side of the gate. With a titbit and making the shushing sound give the Come command. This time, as your dog goes to pass underneath the gate, check him by gently holding him down by the shoulders as he is about to emerge from under it. At exactly this moment give him the Down command. Hold him there for just a few seconds. Follow this immediately with a rewarding titbit before releasing him with the command "That'll do". As he emerges from under the gate, once again go into a knotted-sock frenzy with him with much added praise!

You will then find that after doing this about a dozen or so times, your dog will begin to anticipate the down just prior to reaching the gate. When he does you will quickly realise that you have nearly achieved what you set out to do.

So far you have not actually stood next to your dog and forced him into a down in the traditional way, but left this entirely to the dog himself. He performed the action of his own volition and you followed with the Down command! You put no pressure on the dog in the slightest and he was a willing participant.

As you repeat this you will be able to move gradually away from the gate and stop your dog with just the voice command of Down in mid flow then calling him on again for his titbit, praise and play reward with his knotted sock.

As time progresses you will then be able to call your dog to you using the shushing noise from wherever you happen to be. Within a very short space of time the Instant Down will became part of every day life and of course become an integral part of the Sendaway exercise to be seen shortly.

You have then taught your dog the basics of the Come When Called and the Instant Down whilst on the move in a totally natural manner. There has been no resentment on his part and consequently no hang-ups.

Our training proper has commenced!

If proof were ever needed of the importance of the Instant Down then an incident that occurred when I still had Boots brought it all home to me. I was living in Southampton and had taken Boots down to Southampton Common for a long walk. I entered the common from the Hill Lane End through a gap in the hedge that had been created by people over the years who couldn't be bothered to walk to the main entrance.

Roughly 100 metres in from the hedge is a narrow road that pretty well encircles the common and is used by walkers, maintenance staff and police patrol vehicles. I have previously mentioned Boots' hatred of other dogs. Well, on this particular morning, on reaching the common, I discovered that we had the place to ourselves, or so I thought. Foolishly I let him off his lead the moment we had entered the common. Well Boots, who could spot a fly climbing a wall at a hundred paces, observed a dog well off into the distance, and shot off like a rocket. This in itself didn't overly concern me because I knew he would come back if I called him enough. No, it was the police patrol car on its rounds and heading straight toward the point at where Boots was about to cross the road onto the common that terrified me.

Without even stopping to think I just shouted out DOWN in my loudest voice I could muster and Boots dropped like a stone just a yard or so from the front wheel of the police car. It was only when the car had travelled on for a few more metres did it stop, for the driver had not even seen Boots heading toward disaster. But he had heard my voice right enough. He got out of the car and approached me. 'Here we go,' I thought, 'a lecture about letting my dog run loose,' was about to be unleashed. But no, I was wrong. Instead he congratulated me on having such a well-trained dog and admitted to having not seen him, only stopping because he heard my panic stricken voice commanding Boots to lie down.

Chapter 3

The Sendaway

To complete this training you will need

- A 4" deep stainless steel feed bowl.
- Smaller similar stainless steel or white plastic bowl for a puppy.
- Play toy or titbits.

A typical Sendaway test at an Open or Championship Obedience show

Sendaway areas, or the area or 'box' that the dog is being sent to at shows, can be very confusing. In early Obedience Shows dogs were often sent to nothing other than maybe a ring post, a cloth tied to a ring rope or nothing at all other than a directive to send them in the direction of a tree observed in the far distance.

These days there seems to be such a variety of Sendaways dreamt up by judges that it has become very confusing for the dog. I feel this has overlooked the spirit of the exercise which was to send the dog away from you in a straight line until asked to drop. Very often today the dog is presented with a myriad of markers and detractors ranging from upturned flower-pots and simple peg markers to model windmills and Border Collie shapes cut out of plywood.

Most judges place two markers about a metre apart and some 2 – 3 metres forward of a ring post or back marker. Alternatively they form a 'box' of roughly 1.5 metres square across the far side of the ring. This is where the dog is expected to end up in. Others do similar things but use circular or triangular marked areas. The bottom line is that the Kennel Club is not hard and fast on what a dog should be sent to. You should therefore really train your dog to ignore all markers and simply run straight away from you when he leaves your side on command.

And so, bearing all of this in mind, we commence our Sendaway training.

A really funny thing happened at a show held at Upton Country Park near Slough some years ago. It was Class B and I was competing in it with Drift, my predominantly white collie. The judge, one of the 'old school' who believed that dogs should run toward nothing in the Sendaway test, had tied a Union Jack patterned plastic carrier bag to a ring post by just

Top Tips

- Remember! Teach the basics of the 'Sendaway' as early as possible.

- Remember! Make sure that there are no objects in the path to distract or confuse.

one of its handles. The flag was billowing about like a windsock and w
quite off-putting. I was standing behind a chap with a rather large GS
who was next to go into the ring to compete.

The Sendaway test was the first and the ring steward asked the competit
with the GSD to prepare his dog for the test. The man turned to the stew
ard and asked him what he had to send his dog to? The steward replie
that is was the open carrier bag hanging on the post. The competitor, kee
ing a straight face, looked him straight in the eye and said 'he'll never g
inside that bag, he's much too big!' As you can imagine this brought th
house down but then, that is the humour that goes around the shows.

Anyway, the downside was that this particular competitor's dog failed th
test miserably as he had not been taught to run in a straight line. Instea
he had been trained to look for marked areas to run toward. Because
the array of other distractions he had simply picked up on something ou
side of the ring and headed for it in hope rather than in an assertive ma
ner. Because of my training methods, Drift, on the other hand, roared
without any hesitation in a straight line that took him directly to the bas
of the post that the bag was hung on. Drift and I came second that da

I have always taught my dogs the basics of a Sendaway right from th
moment they are taken from their mothers and placed in their ne
surroundings. I do exactly the same with the older dog. As in all trai
ing, there are other methods that can be applied, but this is the or
that suits me most because it gives the dog the incentive to willing
leave your side and go away from you in a straight line with a certai
amount of verve and determination.

For the Puppy

Put your puppy's food in a stainless steel dish or bowl that has reason
ably high sides. Place the dish on the floor about 2.5 metres away fro
where you are going to send him from. Show your puppy the dish wit
the food in it but prevent him from diving-in. Move your pup backwar
slowly telling him to Look Straight as you do so. You may have your pu
on a lead at this time. If the pup is hungry or interested enough he wi
struggle to get away from you and reach his bowl. The moment yo
have reached your 'launching' position, kneel down and place the pu
partly between your knees. Command him to Wait and Look Straigh
At the same time 'cup' his head in your hands and point him in the direc
tion of his bowl. After a second or two and when you have unclipped th
lead, if he has one, let him go with the command Away or Go.

Top Tips

■ Remember! Teach the
basics of the 'Sendaway' as
early as possible.

■ Remember! Make sure that
there are no objects in the
path to distract or confuse.

your dog's head in your hands
point him in the direction of his
wl.

The normal result is a puppy whose legs are going 'twenty to the dozen' and skidding across the floor in the rush to get to his dish!

Loads of praise. Your pup has completed his first Sendaway.

Repeat this every mealtime as a matter of course, increasing the distance up to about 10-15 paces away, even if it means moving out of the house to do it.

Make sure that there are no objects in the path of the puppy or any obvious visible distractions.

The Older or Rescued Dog

At feeding time place your dog's high-sided dish up the garden path or lawn about 10-15 paces away. Show him the food and restrain him. Moving backwards take him back to his 'launching' position. Stand behind and across him in a somewhat straddling position. As with a pup, put your dog on a lead if you feel more comfortable. Telling him to Look Straight, place your open hands either side of its head and with fingers pointing to the front and covering side distractions from its eyes, command your dog to Wait and Look Straight again.

After a few seconds and only when your dog is looking straight, send him on the command Away or Go. Don't be harsh on anticipation at this stage and don't give him any down commands on reaching his dish, just praise. Repeat over many days or until the dog is totally confident and at ease with your rather strange behaviour!.

The next stage is the same for any age of dog.

The importance of correct bowl placement

When our puppy or older dog is completely confident to go out to his bowl you can put into practice the secret of obtaining a good Sendaway that doesn't stop short when attempting the exercise under ring conditions.

So far you have been able to place the bowl up the garden with some food in it and send him on his way. This has become an integral part of his life. But the Sendaway for both pup and older dog now begins in earnest.

Top Tips

Remember! Always use an easily seen bowl in the early stages of 'Sendaway' training.

Over a period of several weeks gradually lower the dog bowl until it lies flush with the surface of the ground.

I find with Poppi a tennis ball is her 'turn-on'.

Move so that you are stood upright behind your dog and ensure that his body is aligned perfectly in the direction you are about to send him.

The older dog's food bowl should be roughly 15 cms deep. Use an easily seen bowl - not red/blue/green as a dog can not see these colours clearly against a grass background. Stainless Steel or white are ideal.

For the first week continue to keep sending your dog to his bowl, once with his dinner in and about four or five times more with a titbit. If you prefer you can use the knotted sock or play rag that hopefully you would have been continuing to have fun with in-between work and play. I find with Poppi a tennis ball is her 'Turn on'. The commands are the same Wait, Look Straight and Away or Go, but you will now be holding your dog with your hands either side of his head in the wait position for much longer and insisting that he looks straight ahead and concentrates.

Accept nothing less!

At the start of the second week lower the bowl into the ground by a third of its height at a distance of about 20 metres by digging a shallow hole. This will be a formality for your dog as long as the bowl is of a suitable colour and is easily seen. Repeat the whole exercise about five or six times a day. This time remove the hands gradually while continually repeating the command Look Straight. You should still be in a part-straddling position behind the dog. The distance sent to the bowl can be increased as confidence grows.

On the third day of the second week lower the bowl a further one-third into the ground. We are left with one third of the bowl still showing above ground. This is the moment that the dog begins to take more notice and is the most important stage. Keep this part up for a whole week. Continue to start with the hands shielding your dog's eyes from distractions and tell him to Look Straight. Slide your hands back slowly while moving backwards so that you are standing upright behind your dog to ensure that his body is aligned perfectly in the direction you are about to send him. If all is well and your dog is continuing to look straight ahead then send him on his way.

We have now got an understanding going with our dog. Through repetition he already knows that he is going to be rewarded by his dinner,

next stage is to send your dog
you standing alongside him.

a titbit, his play cloth or his ball if he goes out directly to his bowl. He has not been stopped on the way by markers or other distractions. So far it has been a totally rewarding exercise.

Let's keep it that way.

The next stage is to send your dog as you would in a ring situation. This means that you should be stood up alongside of him prior to sending. So the sequence would now be to straddle your dog as before with the hands shielding the eyes, then moving back behind the dog to ensure accuracy and finally to return to his side ready to send.

You then send your dog with the command Away or Go. Your dog will be super keen to run out to his welcoming bowl.

If you feel your older dog or growing puppy is ready to advance to the next level then the bowl is lowered into the ground with only the very top edge of the rim showing. This is the time that concentration really kicks in as the dog, for a moment, begins to scan the area ahead. It already knows in what direction the food bowl lies as you are still channelling his vision with your hands. However, it would be as well to ensure that you have white tape fixed secured to the leading edge of the bowl remaining above ground.

As before, the dog is sent and plenty of praise is given, but only when the bowl is reached, not before.

Finally, the bowl is lowered totally out of sight and the exercise repeated over and over again for a further week, still without downing the dog.

Whilst all this has been going on you will have been training you dog to do an Instant Down as described in Chapter 2, but in a totally different environment and totally detached from the Sendaway. After initially teaching the dog the Instant Down on the spot by passing under an obstruction like a gate, he can then be downed as he is running about in play. The two are not brought together until both are rock-solid and done in complete confidence and in the ring!

To repeat: Never, under any circumstances, down your dog while training the Sendaway. You only ever down your dog in the ring when competing.

Top Tips

Remember! Never fool
our dog by pretending there
a reward when there isn't.

Sometimes there are so many markers at shows that for a poorly trained dog the 'Sendaway' is a nightmare.

You must never allow your dog to think that you have let him down or fooled him. When he is downed in the ring whilst doing a Sendaway, he is downed prior to him reaching his 'bowl' so he never knows that the bowl was not there in the first place. All he knows is that you downed him before reaching it. You must never take away the belief that his bowl and the rewarding titbit or toy were anywhere else but further on. In training the bowl is always there and a practice Sendaway should never be attempted without it.

Markers

I actually hate the very sight of markers because they are a menace and the main reason for Sendaway failures. The very things that should be there to help your dog most are more often the cause of uncertainty, confusion and intimidation. This often results in the handler getting upset with him thus the spiralling fall to constant failure sets in.

But, and it is a reluctant but, they do have there uses. Like a practice scent or difficult retrieve on the show ground prior to entering the ring take advantage of a difficult Sendaway if at all possible.

As I have already mentioned there are so many 'markers' present at shows these days in the form of ring posts, signs, table and chair legs, goal posts and trees, that for the poorly trained dog the Sendaway is a nightmare!

I recommend the purchase and collection of as many markers as possible to have available on the day. Not that the correctly trained dog needs them. But the familiarity of the objects will give your dog an advantage in what often resembles a circus ring.

We've all seen them - the dog that is set up for Sendaway and immediately observes something to the side of the ring that he is convinced he has to run to. Why? Because he has been trained to run to markers and that particular marker rings a bell in his head, that's why! The dog that has never been trained with markers does not have such hang ups about these things. He just relies on you, his handler, to simply set it up correctly to run out straight. You will actually observe dogs that have been trained to run straight sometimes turn their heads to observe something odd, while still running out in a straight line!

Top Tips

■ Remember! Get your dog used to seeing different kinds of markers.

Another good reason for teaching your dog to run straight to nothing is the deadly white markers that are sometimes used. Some judges will use thin white marker poles. These are passable on a dull day but deadly when the sun is shining bright. At close range they are not too bad but from a distance they are very difficult to see. If your dog is marker trained you are in trouble.

If you can, set up the type of Sendaway that is being asked of your dog on any given day and turn it to your advantage, but ONLY if you can set up a near identical test. Make it the same distance, but place the bowl way back beyond the marked area.

Couple this with a very flat dish that you will have amongst your collection of Sendaway apparel and set your plan in action.

Firstly, send your dog to his normal practice Sendaway bowl that you use in daily training but with the same markers in front that are being used in the ring. Make sure the bowl is at least 20 feet back from the markers with NO distractions in the background whatsoever. Do a couple of these, then replace the bowl with the flat dish that is very difficult to see. This is the moment that your dog will become aware of the markers and where your extra training comes into its own. When asked to do the actual test in the ring, your dog will have a huge advantage because he has already been trained to run straight in an overly cluttered ring. He will be reassured by seeing the same markers indicating where his 'bowl' lies. An exception to this is where there are many markers of the same colour scattered around the ring. In those instances just rely on your dog running out straight and send him 'blind'.

It is of the utmost importance that you align your dog straight when setting him up for the sendaway. As he rises from the sit position he will automatically move forward in a straight line. If you have taught your dog to run straight and you set him up crooked, he will run out to the side you pointed him in.

Top Tips

Chapter 4

Attention

Arguably Attention is most important in any training and absolutely crucial if you are to reach the top in this often intensely competitive discipline.

Attention has two main guises - looking and listening. Visual attention, where your dog is sat by your side with his eyes firmly fixed on yours, or at least on your head, is the attention we are striving for at this stage. Of course we can't achieve this without the other coming very much into play.

I will not attempt any form of precision heelwork with my dogs until I have absolute attention - on the spot, and in a quiet location!

Place your dog in the sit position squarely on your left next to a wall.

Lack of authority here on the part of the handler is very often the most serious early mistake that the keen beginner can make in their rush to get on with things. At the end of the day, when you have reached the top level, it is the heelwork that decides who the 'ticket' is going home with. As a general rule all of the top dogs successfully carry out all the remaining main set exercises so good heelwork is of the essence. Heelwork is marked more closely than most exercises and this is where you have to focus your attention when commencing training.

Assuming that you have now chosen your quiet spot, place your dog in the sit position squarely at your left side with the dog between you and a stationary object such as a wall or fence. If your dog is an adult then his toes will be roughly in line with your own and he will be on a lead fixed to either a collar or a check chain.

31

I always train my dogs on a light check chain with no more than a coup of inches free at the end. Not because I wish to hurt my dogs in any wa but I do get a better 'feel' for what I am doing, but this is purely a matte of choice. Leather or nylon half-check collars are also excellent but tr to avoid a standard one-piece collar as they are very negative.

As you are now expecting your dog to be looking up at you and turnir his head into you this puts pressure on his rear end to move out of pos tion. So the placing of the dog alongside a fixed object is a very impo tant part of this exercise. If a dog has never been allowed to s crooked, then so much the better.

If you have an easily assessable pocket on your right hand side for titbits, or one of those waist purses that are very popular these days, all the better. However, if you are beginning your training with a young puppy it would be as well for you to kneel down on both knees and begin this exercise from there.

Now hold a short reasonably taut lead or special short lead in your left hand and position a titbit or play

Cup your dog's muzzle comfortably with your hand and hold head in the correct position.

toy with your right hand mid-way between the dogs eyes and your Give the command Watch Me.

If you are using titbits only give the shushing noise to gain attention immediately before the Watch Me command. If your dog is looking directly upwards at the toy/titbit and is happy to do so, give him the titbit immediately combined with just the correct amount of praise to suit him.

When giving your dog his titbit during Attention Training offer it at a direct point between eye to eye contact with his head still raised and being asked to Watch Me. Do not let your dog drop his head before offering and giving it.

Likewise, if just using a toy, turn it into a rewarding game of pull for a few seconds. Unless your dog is totally besotted with you the chances are that he is not going to be too keen to initially hold his head in this unusual position for too long. The duration has to be gradually increased, as has the praise, both for the comfort of the dog and his understanding of what you are endeavouring to teach him.

I think it most important at this point to emphasise the importance of not forcing the dog to carry his head too far up and too far back. This style has become very popular but could damage a dog's neck, back and hind quarters, particularly if your dog is the excitable type. Be very sensible, it's not a natural position for a dog to take up - and remember, they are supposed to be working in a natural manner so don't over-emphasise!

With dogs that are not keen to hold their heads up like this, I have found that if I actually take off the lead and put my left thumb through the end eye of the check chain, I can then cup the dogs muzzle comfortably into my left hand. This enables me to then gently hold the head in the required position whilst offering the dog his titbits and giving praise.

To be honest, this is actually what I prefer and it suits me most. Don't hurry - it's not a race!

You will find once a dog's head is raised his natural inclination is to come forward and around. In the past I have allowed this to happen as I was quite happy to sort out the straight sit later on. However experience has shown me that it is far better to position the dog's side quarters against a fixed object - as I described and showed at the beginning of the chapter - right from the start. I feel that if he hasn't picked up bad habits early he will have no reason to do wrong in the future.

Once taught I insist that my dogs watch me intensely for some two minutes without taking their eyes off me. This must be in a quiet location. Obedience is hard enough without making life more difficult for oneself or partner, so don't allow distractions at this stage. They will come soon enough so don't worry!

One month after taking over Poppi's training and some six years since competing in Obedience, I entered a show with her at Plymouth DTC and was placed 4th in Novice. The judges written comments of, 'Lovely round with 100% attention,' and 'Over-keenness caused the errors today,' was all I wanted to hear. In her very next show she won the class with that same attention and keenness evident.

Chapter 5

Commencing Basic Primary Heelwork

If you have been patient and your Attention Training has gone well and without too many hiccups you can begin your Basic Primary Heelwork. Like every other exercise take time out beforehand and really consider what you are about to attempt before you start.

Remember, heelwork is all about a partnership - a partnership between you and your dog and partners should never knowingly let each other down, so take time and be patient.

So far, you and your dog have stood rooted to the spot, eyes transfixed on each other with only good vibes emanating. Don't let this change - not for a moment! If things go wrong, return to this happy and confident state for a short period before continuing. Have either titbits or his toy close at hand to regain attention.

Mindless heelwork around an Obedience club hall with other dogs sniffing, snarling and barking may be alright for the experienced dog. But for the young and inexperienced, or unconfident older dog it is a nightmare. Unless you absolutely have to - don't do it! By all means join a local dog club and observe different methods in a club atmosphere without your dog. This would be good preparation for when you can confidently attend. In the meantime keep your dog well away until much more experienced. Once achieved, by all means become a regular member of that club and support them. These clubs provide a very useful service and without them the future outlook for the Obedience Competition could be threatened.

Here we go then

We are going to attempt heelwork at the SLOW pace, in a smallish left-hand circle. The idea being that the dog is being persuaded to work close to the handlers left side, in the position best favoured by the handler i.e. roughly level with the leading leg (left). The head carriage remains the same as in the Attention position. The lead will be kept reasonably tight at all times. With the handler continually turning into the dog, who in turn is on a tight lead, a fixed heelwork position is attained with no drifting on the part of the dog.

Top Tips

Remember! It takes two to do heelwork.

Remember! Always have your dog's toy or titbit to hand.

Once taught correctly, the dog will maintain this position throughout his entire life. It goes without saying that whilst your dog is so receptive to training you have a golden opportunity to work with your dog to Get it Right.

Very shortly we will be looking at definitive footwork patterns and useful tips on how to get the most out of the various 'adjustments' you can make to footwork along the way, but firstly, let's get our dogs into the heelwork mood.

With the dog sat on your left side and paying absolute attention, hold a short tight lead low in your left hand and a titbit or toy in the other in the customary position and give the command heel. Immediately step slowly forward on your left leg, giving the shushing noise if you are using titbits, or watch me if using a toy. Maintain a tight lead and the dog has to come with you. Remember though, if using titbits, you must offer and give the dog his reward after making the shushing noise -

Immediately step forward on your left leg giving the shushing noise if using titbits, or 'watch me' if using a toy.

providing he is watching you. For the first half a dozen efforts, or at least until your dog begins to understand what you are trying to achieve, you will be just creeping forwards a short distance and both probably feeling a little uncomfortable. This is the time for 'over-the-top' praise and encouragement for this first step is the big one and should not be underestimated. Remember though, the initial aim here is to get your dog moving whilst still maintaining 100% attention - accept nothing less. A point to remember and one to be understood, is that when Attention Training was undertaken, the dog was sat at your side. As that first step is taken, the mechanics of your dog's body will change and he will automatically lower his head carriage to a small degree as he stands to commence heelwork. Be very patient - it will return.

As confidence grows increase your pace and in no time at all you will have a willing and happy partner.

Once confident to stride out with you, albeit slowly, increase the distance to two or three paces, but maintain attention and keep moving in a left circle. Giving way here will encourage the dog to 'try it on' later or possibly give way to 'fears' that he may encounter later in life. Regular shushing noises followed by a reward will maintain attention and momentum. If necessary the occasional carefully timed check on the lead will act as a reminder. This, coupled with the command Heel, will soon have your dog confidently striding out by your side. The degree or size of circle is really down to you or, to an extent, what breed of dog you have. I would suggest for starters that it should be about 2.5 metres in diameter, or whatever you feel comfortable with.

Remember, if it goes wrong, return to the stationary mode and regain that Attention on the spot, coupled with a rewarding game and titbit.

If you have achieved 100% Attention beforehand with the dogs head neatly tucked around your upper leg you will find that when you commence this initial heelwork you have a big advantage. Because your dogs head is in this 'wrapped around' position, you almost 'drag' the dog with you by your upper leg as you step off, particularly as you are holding a taut lead. In a way it's like a legitimate extra command which works in your favour. All the more reason to aim for absolute attention with the perfect head position!

Top Tips

■ Remember! It isn't a race.

After the initial success of getting your dog moving and maintaining the correct position coupled with full attention, the left circle can increase in size to whatever you feel comfortable with. See it as a controlled spiralling outward exercise. Eventually, if you have a large enough area to train, such as a local park, the larger circle will simply evolve into virtually straight heelwork. Try not to reach this stage too quickly. Precision and timing lost here could cost you dear later. As confidence grows, increase your pace and in no time at all you will have a happy and willing partner. Your dog's heelwork position will be the envy of many and he will soon be ready to move on to the more advanced stages of basic heelwork. This will include Turns and Footwork which we will concentrate on shortly.

Chapter 6

The Early Recalls, including the Present in Beginners and Novice

Whether you're in Pre-Beginners, Beginners, Novice, or Classes A, B and C, you are going to encounter a Recall.

The 'Come when Called' exercise practiced in Chapter 1 should not be confused with the ring recall as their aims are entirely different and precision wasn't what we were looking for at that time.

A Recall to the front in Pre-Beginners, to a Recall to your left side in Classes A, B & C, plus the recalls in all the Retrieves throughout all of the classes, is evidence of just how important this exercise is.

Strange as it might seem though, we are going to learn the Present before the Beginner or Novice Recall.

Why? Let me explain!

A great deal can happen between you leaving your dog, walking some 10 paces away, turning, then, on command - calling your dog to the front, before finishing. There is also the question of the points it is possible to lose whilst attempting all this. So the aim therefore, is not to lose any of those valuable points.

Young and inquisitive dogs can often lose concentration on their Recall so we don't want to make matters worse than they already could be by the time the Present is required. It is doubly important therefore that the position they take up on reaching the handler, is 'carved in stone' beforehand.

The Present

Stand immediately in front of your dog although he has already presented.

Stand immediately in front of your dog as though he has already presented.

With a titbit in your hand and both hands held in the Recall position, your dog on a taut lead if you prefer, make the shushing noise, coupled with the dog's name and the command Come. With the help of the lead, if you're using one, slowly move backwards, drawing your dog with you and after a metre or so, give the titbit and plenty of praise. Remember when training with titbits, to give a reward often, but only when the job has been done correctly. If, when moving backwards, the dog's backside lifts off the ground more than two or three inches, you are moving too quickly - so slow down! Because you are moving backwards slowly, you are in the unique position of being able to allow the dog to sit when you are ready i.e. whenever his body is aligned correctly. Thus he never learns to sit crooked. You will rarely have to give the sit command as he is already in a semi-crouching position he naturally reverts to this state as you stop.

Once confident and you have increased the distance covered in walking backwards, it can then become snakelike as you move into what I describe as a 'serpentine mode'. This meandering teaches the dog to align himself again properly with the handler. It is particularly useful if, for some reason, your dog has been distracted during his Recall. As before he is only allowed to sit when in the correct position.

Immediately the dog is willing to move back with you then dispose of the lead and just use titbits if you prefer.

Top Tips

■ Remember! Reward often – but only if the exercise has been done correctly.

The Recall

When you are both confident in the Present you can then go about teaching your dog the Recall, initially from one of the very sits that you have just taught whilst teaching the Present.

Firstly, place your dog back onto his lead. Now, giving him the command Wait, not stay, hold a taut lead about 25 cms above the dog's head and move back as far as you can so that the dog is at arms length from you.

Give your dog the command 'Wait', hold a taut lead above his head and move back as far as you can.

Repeat the Wait command, both with voice and combined hand signal as often as you have to. No titbits at this time though, just praise, as we don't want the dog moving forwards to receive them.

Extend further away until waiting, recalling and presenting have been achieved at any distance.

After about half a minute, or when stability has been reached, move the hands to the Recall position and at the same time use the dogs name plus the shushing noise and the command Come. If you have taught the Present correctly, the response will be immediate, with an instant Recall the likely result. Because you will have taught it so well, there is every possibility that your dog will present in the perfect position, but if there is any indication that he will not, step backwards until he is straight before you allow him to sit. In all probability you won't even have to use the lead to encourage the dog towards you.

You have achieved your first Recall and Present

The Present has now been perfected, leaving you with just the Recall from a distance to work on. Once confident to wait at arms length at the end of the lead, remove the lead, and repeat over and over again until the same confidence is achieved with the lead released. This will then extend a further pace away, then another, until Waiting, Recalling and Presenting have been achieved at whatever distance is felt necessary. As in all training however, don't move on to the next exercise until you have perfected your current one.

Remember, the positioning of the hands are very important. Never have them in the Recall position (in front) until you call your dog - and always have that titbit and praise ready to give instantly the exercise has been achieved satisfactorily. Accept nothing less!

Top Tips

■ Remember! Never move on to the next exercise until you have perfected the current one.

Chapter 7

Always keep a knotted sock or other toy about you and use it to have a game at the end of each section of your training.

The Retrieve - Part 1

Although the basics can be initially taught in the form of a game, the Retrieve is nevertheless an exercise that one should treat seriously once underway. It must be carried out methodically and accurately in a working environment.

The Basics

A play rag or knotted sock is ideal as an introduction to the Retrieve. Keep either about your person when teaching all exercises and use it to have a game at the end of each section of your training. A dog that enjoys a game of 'pull' is normally very reluctant to give up his 'toy', so take full advantage and include the command Hold whilst he is doing just that. Whilst your dog is still keen to play and holding his 'toy', give him the recall command and ask him to present in exactly the same way as we practiced earlier. Once completed give him the command Give and take the article from his mouth but don't send him to heel, just have a game.

Moving on from here you can then start playfully throwing his 'toy' about the garden or room whilst giving him the command Hold before finishing the exercise as before.

You have completed your first Basic Retrieve.

Introduction to the Dumbbell

There are two main types of dumbbell in general use

- The rounded central bar type
- The square bar type.

I very much favour the latter and make my own to suit each individual dog.

It is very important to take the breed and size of your dog into consideration when ordering or making a dumbbell. As an example, a typical Border Collie dumbbell should not have a centre-bar width more than around 9 cm and square ends of more than 8 cm square. I'm not trying to preach to the enlightened here but I will explain to the newcomer how I gauge the size of a dumbbell for my individual dogs.

The size of the dumbbell must be taken into account and will differ according to the breed and size of your dog.

Any oversize dumbbell will do for starters so that you can take measurements while the dog is holding one in his mouth. Place an over-sized dumbbell in your dog's mouth and slide it to one side. From the inside of the side touching his cheek measure the width to 2.5 cm beyond his cheek on the other side. In my opinion this is the correct inner width.

If a dog picks up an over-width dumbbell on one side he will not be comfortable and will become distracted from his task of presenting it correctly, often throwing in a crooked present.

Now to the dumbbell ends.

Rotate the dumbbell in your dog's mouth so that the pointed ends of the square ends are directed toward the eyes. A correct sized end would fall short of the eyes by 2.5 cm to be correct. I think that there are two main reasons why dogs 'roll' a dumbbell in their mouths. Firstly that the ends are either too wide and impair vision or, secondly, that a round centre bar allows a dumbbell to roll as they often push it along the grass when picking it up.

At many shows you will see a dog returning with a dumbbell. He keeps lifting his head and re-positioning it in his mouth. In most cases this is because the ends of the dumbbell are too big and he is moving the bell so that the 'flat' end of the square end lies beneath the eye so vision is restored. A square centre bar assists with a pick-up as it does not revolve so easily when rubbing along the grass. Some square dumbbells are angled at 45 degrees as this is the angle many dogs pick up from.

The correct size square ends, correct length, and square bar make for the perfect dumbbell for those main reasons.

Introduce the dumbbell kneeling down and from the side, give the command 'hold' and pop the dumbbell in his mouth.

It is not normally a good idea to just suddenly appear out of the blue with a dumbbell. Leave it lying around your training area well beforehand. Your dog will get accustomed to the sight of it. Let's face it they can be quite fearful looking things to a young dog can't they?

I always introduce my puppies to a dumbbell whilst kneeling or lying down. This is so that they are introduced to it at the same level as they have become accustomed to seeing it lying around during their other training. Bear this in mind.

Once the dumbbell is in your dog's mouth gently raise the lead in your right hand and gently hold it against the central bar of the dumbbell.

Have your dog sat comfortably by your left side with his lead attached, preferably to a fixed leather collar. Keep his head still by holding on to the rear of the collar and give the command Hold. Pop the dumbbell into his mouth for a second or two. Do not let go. Issue the command Give then remove the dumbbell. Follow this with plenty of praise and a titbit if using them. Repeat this about six times, or until obvious confidence shows. If your dog is not keen to open his mouth to receive the dumbbell, gently open it by clasping your left hand around the lower jaw and insert your fingers and thumb either side of the mouth, prising the teeth gently apart. Again the command Hold coupled with plenty of praise is given as you pop it into his mouth.

Now, repeat the whole process again. But this time, once the dumbbell is in your dog's mouth, raise the lead in the right hand and gently hold it against the central bar of the bell so that it prevents the dog from pushing it out as you let it go. All the time you are repeating the command Hold in a happy and encouraging tone and telling him what a good boy he is. Your hand holding the lead will be only just above the dumbbell. Again, only attempt this for a few seconds until confidence has grown. Once confident, the lead can be dropped and the dog left holding the dumbbell until asked to Give. Constant praise is most essential.

Top Tips

 Remember! Leave the dumbbell around to get your dog used to seeing it.

Encourage your dog to pick the dumbbell off the ground by progressively lowering it to the ground.

The next stage

So far, we have given the dumbbell to the dog. Now we have to teach the dog to reach out and take it for himself

Once confidence has been gained, you will find that if you incorporated the dumbbell in play and offered it with the command Hold, he will be eager to take it willingly like his 'toy' beforehand. This is just one method, and an easy one, of persuading the dog to 'reach out' and take his dumbbell from you. Very soon you will be able to revert to a kneeling position and carry on where you left off. Your dog should now stick his head out and hold it when commanded instead of you having to place it into his mouth. Once this has been achieved, start to lower the dumbbell closer to the ground so that your dog is now not only reaching out for it, but also going down for it.

Ultimately you will place it on the ground and your dog will be happy to reach down and pick it up for you. All you need is patience and determination!

Before completing the retrieve exercise, take time out to really consolidate what you have just taught your dog. Get him used to carrying the dumbbell by sitting by your side with it in his mouth. Then get him really confident by doing left-hand circles of heelwork, again with the dumbbell in his mouth.

Things to remember

Like all training the retrieve must be a pleasurable experience for both of you. Retrieve Training allows you the opportunity to have fun with your dog as in these initial stages it should be no more than a serious game. Try to keep it that way whilst working toward the perfection that will be required on entering the ring.

Get him used to the dumbbell by doing left hand circles of heelwork with it in his mouth.

Chapter 8

With your dog sitting on your left side command him to 'Wait', step forward with your right leg.

Encourage your dog to go around your left foot to pick up the dumbbell.

You can ensure a good pick up by placing the dumbbell behind another object.

The Retrieve - Part 2

Fetching, Presenting & Finishing

Once confidence has been gained and your dog sees the dumbbell as a 'toy' rather than a frightening object, you can begin to concentrate on the Fetching, Presenting & Finishing.

Fetching & Presenting

With your dog sitting at your left side and attached to a lead, command him to Wait. Then, take one pace forward with your right foot. Place the dumbbell to the left of your right foot and withdraw your foot. Now, on the command Hold, take one pace forward with your left foot and simultaneously encourage your dog to go around your left foot to pick up the dumbbell from behind. As your dog is picking up the dumbbell, repeat the command Hold and then, as you withdraw your foot, draw the dog to you with the help of the lead into the Present with the command Come. Ensure, with the positioning of the hands, that you attain a high head carriage on presentation. Feel free to use your dog's name prior to the Hold command.

I have endeavoured to teach the Fetch in a very simple and uncompli-cated way so that the dog is actually facing the handler when the dumbbell is picked up. An over-keen dog will often overshoot the dumbbell on the way out in his haste to gather his 'toy' and lose points unnecessarily in the process. Do not step forward on your left foot when initially placing the dumbbell, as this will encourage the dog to come with you, as it is the leading leg. Only use the left foot when ask-ing your dog to retrieve it.

Use your left hand on the lower end of the lead or even the collar to encourage your dog to go around your foot. Once learnt, the left hand can then be used temporarily as a signal when sending your dog out.

I've found an alternative way of ensuring a good pick-up from behind is to place the dumbbell behind an object so that it makes the dog go around before picking it up. Another way to line a dog up for a decent present is to place the dumbbell midway between you and the dog and get him to pick it up and present it on a training recall.

Finishing, or going to Heel for both the Retrieve and the Novice Recall

You may remember that when we tackled the Novice Recall and Present, we didn't finalise the exercise with the Finish. I choose to teach my dogs this exercise once the retrieve has been completed and not before. No particular reason, I just do!

I always teach my dogs the left-hand finish. In fact they don't even know what a right-hand finish is! The left-hand finish, by its very nature, automatically teaches the dog to turn left. It is therefore a great time saver. If you teach your dog the right-hand finish then that's all you are doing. It serves no other purpose.

With your dog sat in the Present position and wearing a suitable collar, give him the command Wait. Then, on a further command of Wait, slide your left hand down into the collar, with the back of the hand against the side of the dog's neck. Hold the collar whilst in this position. On the command of Close, said firmly, together with plenty of verbal encouragement and praise, step back on your right leg. Simultaneously draw your dog back along your left side applying slight anti-clockwise pressure on his collar, thus encouraging him to perform a left-hand turn.

The back of your left hand against the neck of your dog will automatically persuade him to move his hind quarters in this left-handed direction as you draw him backwards and sideways.

Slide your hand into the collar with the back of your hand against your dog's neck. Grasp the collar then step well back on your right leg and draw your dog along your left side.

When the turn is complete your dog will actually begin to move directly backwards as you apply backwards pressure. Release your left hand off the collar at this point and draw the dog forward into the correct heel position with the right hand. Simultaneously return your right foot and place your dog in the sit with your left hand. Give much praise and a titbit. You have completed your first Finish.

With this method of teaching the Finish and combined Left Turn you have to balance up carefully how much pressure - if any - you are going to put on your dog and he must have a suitable collar. When drawing your dog backwards and sideways in the manner described be aware of using just the correct amount of tension as you draw back and twist on the collar. Remember, it's meant to be a hint of pressure - not an all out assault on your dog!

Encouragement as always is your greatest weapon, not heavy-handedness! Be careful not to allow your dog to swing out too far as you draw him sideways and backwards. It is all too easy to create a wide finish. Just be sensible.

You will be surprised at how quickly most dogs pick up the left-handed finish. After very few attempts most dogs start to anticipate and begin turning as you move your left hand down the lead. You know you've cracked it when this happens, It's then just a question of repeating the exercise until dog and handler are as one and you can then use a left hand signal coupled with the command Close. Try the exercise initially without the dog to experience the 'rocking' sensation that is achieved when the right leg is taken backwards and forwards correctly. Remember - be patient!

Once your dog has the idea and is prepared to move into the left-handed finish you can set about doing away with all the aids used so far.

Top Tips

◀ Remember!
ncouragement is your
est tool.

However some dogs take exception to being handled and will actual move away from the handler when the hand goes down to the collar ar do a very wide finish. In this situation you will need further assistance

The perfect solution here is to stand just adjacent to a wall on you left-hand side and encourage your dog to complete a left-hand finis between the wall and you. I find this an excellent method and if applie correctly, foolproof. Just ensure that you leave enough space for you dog to comfortably move in-between to begin with. You can tighten up once the dog is confident.

The perfect end result to a left-handed finish is when your dog's hea goes immediately to your left leg and pivots from this point. To achiev this position involves correct handling on the lead but only once th general concept has been fully understood by him.

What you do is to again have the dog Present to you in the normal accepted way and on a lead held in the right hand, but held down low i the left hand and as level and close to your dog's head as you can. Nov as the dog begins his left-handed finish, simply keep a short taut lea and don't allow his head to leave your left leg. It's a very simple prc cedure that is totally governed by your ability to carry it out correctly

Chapter 9

ou can create a near identical ituation to a garden wall using ywood.

The Right and Right-About turns on the spot

In chapter five I dealt with the basics of commencing heelwork. By this time, if you have stuck solely to the described method of gaining Attention, you will be well up to starting your Novice Heelwork with a vengeance.

It is best to illustrate the correct placing of feet when teaching the turns with the help of drawings. To begin with you will practice the steps on your own and on the spot. Once learnt - enter the dog! With the dog, the right-hand turn is to be taught in a 'corner', which you will have either constructed, or already have available to prevent the dog from swinging out. A clear corner in your house is also ideal, as long as your dog is comfortable in either this situation. Obviously when attempting this on your own, the wall or corner is of no importance.

ith your dog on a short lead ake sure that the gap between e dog and the wall is enough for m to negotiate the turn.

Outside I find a garden retaining wall of around two feet in height perfect, although a near identical situation can be created quite easily using plywood or other such sheet material.

Here we go then - the Right-Turn without your dog

Step 1   Both feet together.
Step 2   Place your left foot to form a T
Step 3   Place your right foot alongside your left foot

Repeat over and over until confident.

Right turn on the spot

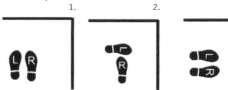

With Your Dog

Place your dog in sitting position on your left side on a short lead.

ace your left foot in the 'T' posi- on and draw your dog around our leg with the lead.

The gap between the front of your dog and the wall, fence or purpose made corner should just be enough to enable the dog to manoeuvre. Holding a short taut lead, use the dogs name to gain attention. Give an assertive Watch Me, Heel command. Place your left foot in the 'T' position and begin to draw your dog around your leg with the lead. Complete the movement as previously practiced with another command Heel and as you bring your feet together, place the dog firmly into the sit with the command Sit. Obviously the barrier to the left and to the front of the dog will prevent his rear end drifting out as you turn. Placing him into the sitting position will stop him from making any forward movement as you complete the exercise.

The Right-Turn with extended heelwork

Many judges will try and catch you out by ordering a halt immediately after a turn. However, the majority of turns will be followed by straight heelwork. This is a very simple procedure, but nevertheless must be accomplished by taking a sensible approach regarding foot work.

As we have just seen, the handler's two feet come together at the end of the right-turn on the spot, but when continuing straight on into heelwork in the ring, this will almost certainly be penalised. By bringing your feet together and planting them on the ground together, you will have been deemed to have ceased working so when continuing on we have to make allowances for this.

To start with when training a young puppy or our older dog it is best to bring the feet together as described on the right-turn to help the dog to keep up. Then step out of the turn on the left leg. Remember the left foot and leg always point the way forward in training!

Once learnt and confident to carry out the move it is simply a case of completing the T shape with the left foot then simply striding out with you right thus eliminating the need to bring the two feet together.

Many years ago a good friend introduced me to a decent footwork pattern. It isn't quite the same as I use now but close enough. Ron was a great character and used to make me cry with laughter at how he used to learn his heelwork patterns while at work. He used to work in a very large storage facility where they had countless rows of walkways beside huge stacking bays. Much to the amusement of his work-mates he used to 'walk' up and down the rows, practising his footwork while carrying box upon box of goods for storage. Often, as he got carried away with what he was doing, the foreman would find him huge distances away from where he was actually supposed to be, so in haste, he would deposit something like a box of baked beans on a shelving unit meant for ladies' 'essentials' and beat a hasty retreat before he got rumbled.

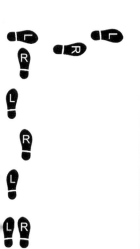

s both you and your dog's
nfidence grows step out of
ur right turns on your right leg.

Putting it all together during heelwork

Once fully conversant with the right-turn on the spot, heelwork proper can commence. Starting with the, by now, well established large left-handed circle at normal pace and with your dog's full attention and holding a play toy or titbit, give the dog's name followed by the Watch Me and Heel command and move off. Starting as if you're going into a large left-hand circle, revert almost immediately into straight line heelwork, then, once settled into a nice rhythm, prepare for your very first right-hand turn.

When into your stride and when you feel comfortable, without slowing, go into your right turn. Ensure you keep a taut lead and give plenty of encouragement.

To start with bring your feet together as you complete the turn as already explained. This allows your dog time to keep up with you and compose himself before striding out of the turn on your left foot. You can now keep in a straight line and throw in a turn whenever you feel comfortable. Try not to always turn in a natural corner. Remember when in the ring 'corners' can come anywhere or at any time. Introduce the sit at the end of your heelwork placing the dog into the position every time while stopping on your left foot. At this stage don't leave it to chance.

Practice this periodically over many days. As both you and your dog's confidence grows step out of your right turns on you right leg, rather than bring your feet together and come out on your left. If you have been patient you will notice no hesitation on the part of your dog as your forward moving body, combined with a taut lead, will allow the whole thing to flow. You are now well on your way to having your dog demonstrating super stylish heelwork.

Remember to always have your play sock, toy or titbit with you at all times. At those moments of hesitation, confusion or uncertainty, or when you need a break, either one is essential to return to that 'feel good factor' so important when training.

Top Tips

◼ Remember! In moments
f hesitation, confusion or
ncertainty – play a game.

The Right-About Turn on the Spot

The right about turn is again best explained by the use of a diagram

- Stand with your feet together in the corner without your dog
- Place your left foot across the front of your right foot to form a T shape pointing toward the right. If you find this difficult an L shape will suffice.
- Then reverse your right foot to form a reverse T or L with your right foot pointing in the opposite direction to its previous position
- Finally bring your left foot alongside your right foot.

You have completed the Right-About Turn. As always practice until perfect without the dog. Don't worry, in time and with practice, all these footwork patterns will become second nature to you.

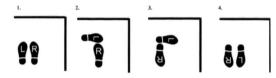

With your dog

Once confident you can again put this into practice with your dog exactly the same manner as before with the right turn, both in the training box and in heelwork proper. Remember, keep it happy.

The importance of good Halts

It is important that when you come to a Halt in training and also your lower classes in the ring, that you always plant your left foot last alongside your right foot. As the left leg is the leading leg it indicates to the dog that you are halting and he is expected to sit as you do so. View this as a free extra command in the early days. However, when competing in the more advanced classes you will be expected to halt on whatever leg you are on at the time.

The Right-About Turn on the move

The Right-About turn on the move is somewhat different. Instead of bringing your feet together as you come out of the turn, you stride straight out on your left foot. You will be aware that you come out of the turn on exactly the same track that you were on before turning.

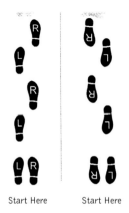

Start Here   Start Here

Finish, bringing dog
to your side and
placing into a sit

Step back on
right foot and
draw dog back
alongside of
you.

Start

The Left-Turn on the spot

For many handlers the left turn in the ring is possibly the one move that causes most concern. But if you follow a set pattern it is really no harder than a standard right turn. As before, it is best practiced on the spot first without your dog. At first this will seem a little odd. I not only turn left but step backwards. This ensures my dog learns to turn left as well.

- With your two feet together plant your left foot into an L shape.
- Then leaving your left foot where it is, bring your right foot directly back one pace and feel your left heel rock as you lean backwards.
- Let your left foot roll back into place and bring your right foot up to and alongside.

You will have already worked out, I'm sure, that what we did in the mid section of the pattern was to step back just as we did when teaching our dog the left-handed finish during the retrieve exercise in Chapter two. Knowing we have already done this is going to make our left turns on the spot very simple to teach indeed.

With your dog sat by your side and on a lead,

- Place your left foot across the front of your right foot
- As you step back on the right foot, draw your dog to the side and behind you with the command Close. Ensure that you bring it right back until you can feel your left heel pivoting on the ground underneath it.
- Then, as you draw your dog up alongside of you, bring your right foot back and place it next to your left foot.

You have completed a perfect left-turn on the spot with your dog. If you find your dog needs speeding up try placing the hand inside the collar and use anti clockwise motion like we used in Chapter two when Finishing.

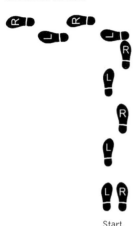

Start

The Left-Turn on the move

The Left-Turn on the move is very straightforward. Whilst you are build-
ing up the confidence you can still step back on that right foot and drag
your dog back on the command Close, before walking out of the turn b
striding straight out on it.

The Left-About Turn on the spot

Once more a very simple manoeuvre when doing this on the spot. How
ever it's more difficult when on the move where variations of one kir
or another often take place! Again, thoroughly practice without th
dog beforehand.

Left about turn on the spot

1.   2.   3.   4.

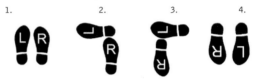

The Left-About Turn on the move

Left about turn on the move

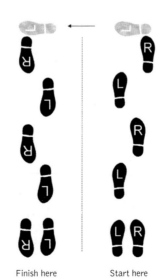

Finish here   Start here

The turn that everybody dread
but still has to learn is the lef
about turn on the move. As in th
left-about turn on the spot, yo
will find that if you go over an
over this pattern without you
dog, you will soon get to kno
what your limitations are an
how close you can comfortab
get to the ideal footwork patter
As long as you are not bringin
your feet directly together at an
given time you will not b
penalised for 'stopping'.

Chapter 10

Test A, B and C Recalls

After the Novice style recalls the next recall you will encounter will be the one in Test A. Here your dog no longer joins in the Present to the front. Instead he presents to your left side when you are walking at a normal pace. This is also the same in Test B and Test C. But in these instances, during the recall part of the Sendaway, your dog will be in the down position and not the sit. When in the ring I also leave my dogs in the down for the Test A recall, but train the recall initially from the sit. Permitted recall commands are also different between classes A, B & C and are:-

Test A.

- Simultaneous command and signal will be permitted.
- Remember that you can use your dog's name as you command and signal as well, EG "Poppi, Heel", while simultaneously raising your arm.

(Your dog's name is free and not considered a command)

Test B.

- One command by voice or signal only. EG "Poppi", while simultaneously raising your arm or by giving the command Heel or Close.

(Again your dog's name is a free command)

Test C.

- As Test B.

Top Tips

Remember! Letting your
⬤g run across your path
⊔st be avoided at all costs.

I leave the teaching of the more advanced recalls until the basic heelwork has been taught and has reached a satisfactory standard. This is because certain parts of this exercise involve working on the spot and a distinction has to be drawn between this and heelwork on the spot as at times they are very similar.

These advanced recalls are very simple to teach but they must be carried out methodically as the hand signals are very important.

During these recalls your dog will always come into your left-hand sid
This is fine when joining up with you in a straight line, but not so easy f
the dog when having to approach from a different angle. Running acro
the face of the handler is a serious fault and must be avoided at all cost

The Recall from behind

Sit your dog by your side attached to a 1.5 metre training lead. Ho
the lead in your right hand and a titbit in your left. Command him
Wait and take two paces forward leading with your right leg. As yc
place your left foot on to the ground on the second stride, raise your le
arm out directly to the left at shoulder height and simultaneously ca
your dog to heel with the command (dogs name) Heel.

As you do this, check and draw him to your side on the lead with yc
right hand while dropping your left hand back into the normal hee
work position. As he reaches your side, give him the Watch Me con
mand to reinstate attention and take three or four more strides befo
halting on your left foot and rewarding your dog with the titbit. Don'
whatever you do, give the dog a titbit as he reaches your side. Th
merely encourages your dog to jump up. Wait until you have come
a halt after a couple more strides.

Repeat this four or five times and when happy with the outcome th
lead can be dispensed with and the exercise practiced until perfec
Once the straight recall from behind has been perfected at this sho
range then it can be increased in distance as confidence grows ar
finally recalled from the down position.

The Recall from the left-hand side

Place your dog sitting on your left-hand side and on a suitable leng
lead held in the right hand. Take one pace forward on your right fo
giving your dog the Wait command. Then go immediately into a lef
turn. As you stride out of the turn raise your left arm out directly
the left at shoulder height and simultaneously call your dog to he
with the Heel command. Bring your arm down immediately so tha
your hand is now in the normal heelwork position and holding a titbi
As in the straight line recall from behind, check the dog on the lead ar
draw him into your side then take a few more paces before halting ar
rewarding with the titbit.

Once the straight recall from
behind has been perfected at short
range keep increasing the distance.

Practice this over and over and increase the distance away from your dog before recalling him directly to your left-hand side and ultimately from the down position rather than the sit.

The Opposite side Recall

The most difficult of all the recalls to perfect is the one where the dog approaches from the opposite side IE the right side. He must learn to pass behind you not in front of you. Again, like all the other recalls this is best trained in a small area and in close proximity to you dog.

With your dog sat at your left side and on a suitable lead held in the right hand give him the command Wait. Leave your dog where he is, turn right on the spot and take one pace forward on your right foot and come to a halt. At this point the lead will run across you to the left and behind to your dog. On the command (dog's name), Heel or Close and while extending your left arm behind you at shoulder level, stride out on your left leg and draw your dog into position by your side. As he joins up with you into the perfect heelwork position give him the command Watch Me and continue to stride out for a further few metres before halting. You will of course have had a titbit ready in your left hand.

Repeat this over and over until confident to practice without a lead.

It is this arm signal from behind that is going to instill into your dog that he has to approach you from behind.

Then, leaving you dog in position as before, take three paces forward and three to the right before calling your dog to your side. Don't forget to use all your commands and, most importantly, raise your left arm behind you at shoulder level. It is this arm signal behind you that is going to instill into your dog that he has to approach you from behind and not cut across the front of you. Once you are confident in your dog's ability to carry out this exercise flawlessly, he can start from the down position in preparation for ring work. Here you will have to rely on the dog's name and arm signal, depending on whether or not you are working classes A, B, or C.

There is nothing to stop you training by turning the top half of your body to the left to overemphasise the action.

When first teaching your dog to come into your left side and raising your arm as a signal there is nothing to stop you in training from turning your body to the left to over-emphasise the action and really encourage your dog to your side with plenty of verbal commands. This is particularly helpful when recalling your dog when he is positioned on the right of you prior to being called. It won't take a dog very long to understand what you are asking of him but any extra help in training is always advisable. If uncertainty is displayed by your dog don't forget to use titbits and a play rag.

Chapter 11

Scent Discrimination

Often described as 'natural' for the dog to learn, the teaching of scent discrimination must still be taught in a methodical and precise way. True, there is very little you can teach a dog with regard to taking scent. But there is a great deal you can do to control how he goes about the method of seeking out an object or cloth that has been purposely scented.

I think that Scent Training ideally starts at puppy-hood with a knotted-up sock. This is carried about my person and is closely connected with teaching a pup the basics of the Retrieve. As we have seen in many of the preceding chapters, the sock is introduced at times of play and as a confidence booster when things don't always go according to plan!

Early Beginnings

For scent, it is first introduced through play whilst out on a walk, or when in the park or the garden. Begin by just playing a game of 'tug' with your dog as you walk along or even when you're sat down. I've

trained many dogs over the years, both in Obedience and for sheep work and have never had one yet that didn't like to play with a knotted sock! It is part of their upbringing and something we all do at some time or in one way or another. In fact, for most of us, it begins with the young pup tugging at out trouser bottoms and at times, to a breeder, it almost seems inbred!

Top Tips

What I do is to have a game of tug then ask my dog to Give me the sock. I then say something like "That'll do" to emphasise that the game is over and just carry on walking. After a metre or two and without my dog noticing, I will drop the sock into the grass behind me and walk on for maybe ten metres more.

I will then turn to my dog in an excited manner and say, "Hey, where your sock? What have you done with it?" I use the command Find and walk back a little way with the dog in a sort of game of 'whos going to find the sock first.'

This has the immediate effect of firing the dog up and sets his mind int working mode where he becomes much more receptive to learning When the sock has been found and the dog comes back to you with h 'prize' resist having a game of tug. Treat this like a recall and mak him sit correctly in front of you and let him give the toy to you withou mouthing on the command Give.

You can then repeat it but this time let your dog go back, on his own, t find the sock. You just give all the verbal encouragement you can muste

This time let him go and find his sock on his own.

Moving on

I much prefer to start this exercise serious on a flat, well cut, grassy area that ha edges that are much rougher, or what th grass cutter has missed and is just lon enough to conceal an object. I like to 'pitc and roll' with my dogs so find this a love exercise to teach as you are in effect com peting with each other to see who is goin to find the sock first!

With your dog tugging away at the soc and you encouraging him to Hold give th command to Give and ask him to let g of it. When he does, toss it down onto th ground a couple of metres away in an excited manner and ask him t Fetch.

Your dogs first reaction will be to dive after it. When he does and a he picks it up just give him the command Hold and ask him to preser it to you in the customary 'Present' position that we learnt when teach ing him to retrieve the dumbbell. Your dog will then automaticall associate this Present with the Retrieve Present where he gave up th dumbbell afterwards. By asking him to Give, he will not hang on t the sock to carry on with the tugging game!

This exercise should be repeated four or five times but only as long as your dog stays keen and is happy to continue. This should not be a problem as it is his 'tuggie' you are using. Remember - keep it happy at all times!

Now you need to extend this exercise and teach your dog to actually use his nose rather than his eyes to seek out the sock. This is what you do:-

- ■ Sit your dog by your side as you would in preparation for the Retrieve.
- ■ Command him to Wait and throw the sock right up to, but short of, the longer grass.
- ■ Command him to Fetch and Hold in the normal way as he does it.
- ■ Do this a further three or four times and really make a big fuss of the dog when he completes each 'retrieve'.

Now the really serious part of this exercise begins

As before sit your dog by your side and command him to Wait. This time throw the sock just into the rough grass and make sure he is watching it. After the briefest of pauses give him the command Find and let him go. You follow shortly behind.

The dog should be so keen to go find the sock that he probably does not even register that you have used a new command (find) and that you have followed him out, especially as you allowed him to go out so quickly. To rectify that keep using the command Find as he is searching in a very encouraging way. This will spur your dog on to find his sock even quicker because he will believe you are trying to beat him to it!

What I actually do is to follow my dog out and say things like, "Where is it?" and "I'm gonna find it first" in a really excited tone. This of course makes the dog try even harder. It also builds confidence and makes him realise that whatever happens you are with him every step of the way. And so you should be, you are partners.

This time of course he cannot see the sock but knows full well the direction it has gone in. If you have been sensible you won't have thrown it too far into the long grass so he will quickly find it. This time, for the first time, your dog will begin to use his nose to seek if he hasn't spotted where it landed. When he finds it your dog would have

Remember! Before throw-
your sock in to the long
ss clear any other objects
t of the way.

completed his very first scer
Lavish praise should be giv
out leaving the dog in r
doubt what a clever boy he h
been.

It is of the utmost importan
that before throwing the so
into the long grass you ha

If no long grass is available you can improvise by throwing the toy behind familiar objects.

completely cleared the area of any other objects that may be lyi
around undetected!

Things tend to escalate from here quite quickly. You repeat the exerci
three of four times a day into the long grass during the next few day
each time throwing the sock to slightly different areas until the sight
'retrieve' becomes a thing of the past. You can also 'hide' the sock
placing it behind familiar objects so that he has to lean to search ever
where. This is particularly useful if you have no long grass to practice

Once your dog has fully mastered this you can move onto the next ste
Now you throw the sock but don't let your dog see where it lands. Th
can be achieved by you both about-turning on the spot and tossing t
sock into the long grass behind you.

Keep throwing the same sock behind you for a while and using the cor
mand of Find to send your dog about his business. When confide
that you have gone as far as you can with this begin to use other clot
or objects that only you have handled, or at least only have your sce
on them.

You can then begin to introduce other objects at the same time as t
knotted sock but only after making sure that you have pinned them
the ground securely. Wear fresh unscented rubber gloves for doing th
and only use objects that you can spike to the ground and have no loo
corners to lift up, such as 15 cm long pieces of 1 x 1 wood or a wall ti
for example.

Discriminating between cloths

Finding a particularly scented cloth amongst other cloths is of course the main objective of the scent test and something that has to be well thought out beforehand. Concentration for your dog is of the utmost importance and is one of those occasions that I believe when you should resort to your 'quiet' area to begin this exercise with.

I don't mess around with training my dogs on just one other cloth. I would rather not allow them the opportunity to bring anything else back other than the correct cloth at this stage. Of course this means giving a lot of thought to your training and making sure that cloths that you wish to remain untouched are firmly secured to the ground.

I will tackle this shortly. But first the main secret to successfully teaching your dog to discriminate between cloths is about how you as a handler take scent from a cloth before giving it to your dog. So many people do this completely the wrong way and end up with dogs who are totally confused in this test but are otherwise super working dogs.

My next advice to you could be one of the most important bits of advice you will ever be given so digest it well.

Over the years I have noticed that the majority of handlers about to enter the ring to work the scent test in classes A & B put their scent onto a cloth with both hands. This is so wrong and such a simple act should be considered very carefully.

Now just think about what they have done?

They have taken a cloth and rubbed it between both hands. By doing this they have not only put their scent onto the cloth but they have also put the scent of the cloth onto their hands.

Now a dog is not stupid. If he doesn't know what his owner smells like then he never will, so they zero in on the smell of the cloth because it is a new and interesting smell.

You must remember that cloths washed in detergent all carry a very similar smell so the fact that the cloths may belong to the club, the judge or Joe Bloggs is irrelevant.

What happens is that you scrunch up or wipe the cloth in both hands, offer your hand to the dog to smell and he very often picks up the first cloth he comes to! Why? Because that is exactly what you have asked him to do - find the smell you had on your hand which came off the cloth.

So this is what you do for A and B in the ring and in training.

Firstly you rub your hands together well. You then pick up the cloth in your left hand, scrunch it all up in your left hand only and offer the dog scent with your right hand only. Obviously make sure that once you have taken the scent on your left hand you do not touch your right hand with it! What you have done is only given the dog your scent and not the scent of the cloth!

Training with a scent pattern

Nail the cloths to the ground about I metre apart.

A clear metre gives you the opportunity to take your dog out on a lead and investigate each cloth.

As I have already stated I train scent on more than just one other cloth but make sure that the blanks are all secured to the ground. I will start with six cloths in a straight line but will gradually add more for complex patterns.

I find a spot that is not regularly trodden on, especially not by me. Using 10 cm round wire nails with flat heads I nail the cloths to the ground 1 metre apart by each of their corners. Try not to place them closer than 1 metre as this will make a dog more likely to hurry to get to one cloth after another as they will all be giving off a scent, albeit virtually the same scent. This clear metre between the cloths gives you the opportunity to take your dog out on a lead and educate him into investigating each cloth completely before asking him to move on to the next. This brings me nicely to the next step.

uietly drop the cloth down on the
ound without your dog noticing.

I never place the cloth to be collected at the beginning of the line. For a dog new to scent this would be a bad move as it teaches him nothing other than to be lazy. It is much better to place the cloth at the end of the line so that he has to examine all the others first and is therefore given the chance to reject them.

After laying out the line and securing the blank cloths to the ground sit your dog by your side on a short lead. In your pocket have the cloth that you are going to ask your dog to find. Don't place this in the line at the moment as you are going to spend time with the other cloths first and you want the scent to be 'hot' when you finally arrive at it.

With the dog sitting by your side offer the flat of your right hand to your dog's nose. If he investigates your hand then just cup it around his nose for a second or two while commanding the dog to Find otherwise just let him scent the air.

Then again on the command Find, walk your dog up to the first secured blank cloth and keeping a slight tension on the lead show him the cloth and ask him to investigate it. Make it almost a bit of a game but with serious undertones and if he should try to nip at it just say "No" quietly and move on to the next cloth in the line where you repeat the command Find again.

Top Tips

■ Remember! Never put
our scented cloth at the start
f the line.

If the dog shows more than a passing interest continue to just quietly say no and check it back lightly on the lead. The interest in the blank cloth won't be because it has your scent on it but simply because it is there and needs investigating. You have made a good start and the dog is reacting exactly as he should.

So you work the whole line like this remembering to give praise as he moves on from each cloth. Now as you approach the last cloth in the line quietly remove the hidden cloth from your pocket. While facing the line you have just come down drop the cloth on the ground behind you without your dog noticing.

Although not seeing it your dog will almost certainly pick up the scent of the charged-up cloth and home in on it straight away. If he does then the moment he picks it up command him to Hold and Come and get him to present it to you there and then.

The reason for doing this is that you can sort out any mouthing or 'killing' of the cloth immediately, do not wait until getting back to the start before doing something about it. Don't forget to get yourself into a position to allow the dog to present correctly with the cloth before taking it. You can do this by walking backwards if need be as we did in earlier training.

If your dog does mouth the cloth then just sit him in front of you as if he had already presented and pop the cloth into his mouth using the Hold command. As the excitement of the scent searching is now over the chances are that he will be perfect again. Don't worry about this as it is perfectly normal for a young dog to behave in this way. Just throw the cloth to the ground and ask your dog to retrieve it as normal and work on the present and any possible mouthing if it occurs.

Many years ago I was judging a Class A and a competitor came in to attempt scent. The dog did a perfectly controlled scent but through inexperience mouthed terribly on the way back. On being instructed to 'take it' by the steward the owner bent over to take the cloth only to find that the dog had swallowed it! The steward never noticed and asked the person to finish their dog and to place the cloth in the plastic carrier bag hung on a ring post on the way out of the ring, which of course he did!!

This should only be a temporary relapse on the dogs part, but if it continued to mouth because of excitement practice this exercise over and over at another time and not over the scent area or during scent training.

Repeat the scent discrimination training as described for the next few days. Slowly you will find less and less interest will be shown in the secured items as your dog gets to realise that sooner or later he will come across your scented cloth and have the satisfaction of bringing it back to you. You will of course show your appreciation in the usual way. During this time you can place the 'hot cloth' in various places alongside the line but 1 metre off to the side. This reinforces in your dog's mind that he will have to search out a cloth that doesn't conform to a set pattern and extends his thinking to the next level which involves a more complex pattern.

The next move is to again go up the line with your dog but without the lead attached. This time, stay just behind the dog and reassure him when things are going right. If you had previously carried out your initial scent training with a knotted sock you will find that working the line successfully comes very quickly and you are not likely to encounter too many problems. Like all training it's a question of taking your time and not moving on to the next stage without consolidating the training already undertaken.

Make haste slowly!

In no time at all you will be able to place the scented cloth anywhere within the line and as long as you recall your dog the moment he picks up the cloth he will have no reason to even think about searching further. I don't like to see dogs finding the correct cloth early then wandering around with it while checking the others because they haven't been taught to return immediately.

Top Tips

■ Remember! Make haste slowly.

Giving Scent in Test C

We are now ready to move on to C now. Remember up until now you have offered your dog scent with your bare hand. Within reason, keep it that way.

Observe how the judge scents up the two cloths as some only rub one side. When you are given one, rub it thoroughly in both hands but ensuring that you cover all of your fingers on your right hand. Face your dog towards the pattern and, when given the go ahead, hold the cloth between thumb and forefinger in each hand. Drape it in front of your dog's nose so that he puts his nose out to smell it. Just in case the judge may have only scented one side of the cloth offer your dog both sides. It is not vital that he touches it although it is preferable but you must be aware that he has noticed it. Finally, scrunch the cloth in your right hand only and offer the scent as you did in B with that hand. You don't need to make a meal of this final scenting, but send him on the command of Find. As before your dog is fully aware of what you smell like and because of that will recognise a strange scent immediately and go out with that last thought in his mind.

Chapter 12

Advanced Heelwork

Changes of Pace

Changes of pace in Class C are carried out on the move and should be fluent with no discernible body signals other than the motion of either speeding up your movements or slowing them down and other than a single command or signal when you commence heelwork from the halt, changes of pace must be carried out without any verbal encouragement or physical signals whatsoever.

In Class B, where the change of pace is from the halt position, you have the opportunity to use either your voice or physical signals at the start of each new pace.

When training for Change of Pace, I never remove the lead from my dogs until competing in the ring. I recall the words of the 'maestro,' the late Charlie Wyant, who always said that if a dog was 'never allowed to go wrong,' then it wouldn't know how to. How true!

That is exactly the position I take up when teaching Change of Pace. To ensure that it cannot go wrong never give your dog the opportunity to drift, lag, jump, surge or get over-excited by keeping him on a lead.

As in the early Primary Heelwork chapter I teach all paces on a taut lead where I have complete control. I use all the aids available; play rag, toys, tit-bit's, voice and signals, but all the while I am not allowing the dog to move even fractionally out of position.

Failure to do this will at some stage allow the dog the opportunity to commit one of the above five sins. Once realising he can get away with slight aberrations without correcting he will be in a position to repeat this at any time, and most certainly will!

Even if you are one of those handlers gifted with natural balance and superb footwork, there will always be a time in training when you waver or stumble on rough terrain causing your dog to drift off your leg if not affixed to a taut lead.

A question often asked is, 'How fast is fast and how slow is slow?'

Top Tips

■ Remember! Always end your training session with a game.

71

I always think that as a sensible rule of thumb, slow pace should be carried out at half the speed of your normal pace and fast pace twice the speed of your normal pace. Some handlers seem to be painfully slow in slow pace, while others in fast pace run around like their pants are on fire!

Common sense should prevail here and after watching the top handlers working in the ring at three or four shows you will soon realise what is regarded as 'sensible' in the pace department.

In training, the transition from one pace to another in your C work should always be accompanied by the correct verbal command. In changing from normal to slow pace, for instance, I use the word "Slow" and added to this, check back on the lead as a further aid.

When moving from slow or normal pace to fast pace I, unsurprisingly, use the command "Fast," but this time give a slight forward check on the lead as my additional aid. Although in the ring you will have to change pace on whatever leg you are on at the time you must, in train-ing, give your dog as much help as is possible. I recommend that you only change pace as you stride out on your left leg. Being the leading leg and used so much in earlier training this will be familiar and bene-ficial to your dog and teaches you, as the handler, to be extra precise.

Advanced Sit, Stand and Down

By the time you have reached the stage of teaching your dog the Advanced Sit, Stand and Down, he should be confident in his work and capable of tackling this 'interruption' in his normal heelwork. In addi-tion he would, of course, have already learnt to sit, stand and lie down in his normal stay exercises, seen in Chapter 13, so it won't be such a diversion from his daily training regime.

Positions on the move must be carried out precisely and in a clean-cut way and look natural to the normal flow of the heelwork. Any devia-tion from this through uncertainty by either dog or handler will be patently obvious to a judge and marked down accordingly.

The easiest part is the stand position at a slow pace and off the lead and this is where I like to start my ASSD training. It is the least obtru-sive of the exercises and suggests to your dog that heelwork isn't all about turns. This makes his attention span longer because he is antic-ipating a position being thrown in at any time.

Using the flat of your hand touch his nose and say the command 'Stand'.

When he stops give the 'Stand' command and hold up your left hand as a signal.

After completing half the circle, turn to partly face your dog to emphasise the 'Stand' command.

Don't walk too close to your dog when you go past him.

Have titbits or a play rag about your person and easily accessible at all times.

The Stand Position

With your dog doing heelwork at a slow pace and off the lead, turn into a left handed circle of around 10 metres in diameter. When comfortable, using the flat of your left hand place it in front and touching your dogs nose. At the same time give the command Stand. As the palm of your hand touches his nose and as you give the command Stand, apply backward pressure on the nose to just keep the dog in check. For a dog previously trained to stand on the spot this is a really easy method of teaching this manoeuvre.

As the dog stops, it won't be immediate to start with, keep giving the Stand command and hold up your left hand as a signal. Continue your left circle without the dog and at a slow pace. After completing about half a circle turn to partly face your dog to really emphasise the Stand command. By this stage of his training he should have gained the confidence to stand on the spot for as mind.

long as he is asked to. The hand signal just reinforces things. As your circular pattern brings you back to your dog's side just give another Stand command and continue with the circular heelwork pattern on your own. If there is uncertainty on the part of the dog and he tries to join up with you just apply the backward palm pressure as before.

Keep him on the spot for about two or three revolutions, then, as you go passed him the next time, have your titbit or play rag ready in your left hand. On the excited command Heel, bring your dog back to your side and continue with straight heelwork. Do this for a few yards at slow pace before changing to normal pace for a few more yards before placing your dog into a sit at the end of it. Naturally you will end the training session with a titbit and a great game of tug.

After leaving your dog in either the stand, sit or down DON'T walk too close to him when you go past him. This could encourage anticipation. Only come in close on collection.

Apply slight backward pressure on the lead to encourage a fast sit.

Stepping out to the right, drop the lead and keep your dog on the spot with as many 'sit and Wait' commands as felt necessary and continue your left-hand circle.

Partly turn to face your dog and offer your right hand, palm up, as a wait signal and give the command 'Wait'.

Leave a gap of around 20 cms, just enough to apply slight palm pressure to your dog's nose if needed. Don't use your dog's name before the pick-up command 'Heel.' Your dog must come to your side on the position command and not on his name. I would strongly suggest you ONLY use the Heel command on pick-up.

The next stage is to increase your pace and diameter of the left-handed circle. Again, with your dog off the lead, go into a slow left-handed circle. This time expand the diameter to about 20 metres. After one circumference increase your pace to normal and, when ready, do exactly the same as before with the backward movement of the hand and the Stand command. This time though be a bit more assertive so that it is more of a firm check or bop on the nose rather then a gentle backward push.

If applied correctly this makes the dog stop on the spot. In future the simple motion of the left hand sweeping across the face of the dog without touching it will have him stopping in his tracks without a further need to touch him. Obviously if you have a problem with you dog not stopping abruptly enough in the future just give him the occasional reminder with the flat of the hand on the nose.

The Sit Position

A good starting point for the sit position is the already learnt sit position used at the end of heelwork. Clip a short 'handled' lead on to your dog so that when released from your hand during the exercise it hangs from the dog's collar without touching the ground.

With your dog on this short lead go into a left-handed circle at slow pace, when ready, come to a halt. As a matter of course your, by now well trained dog, will sit the moment you come to a standstill. However, for the benefit of this exercise, apply backward pressure on the lead to encourage a fast sit. As you do this throw in a firm Sit command. Then, as you repeat the Sit command, step out with your right foot to the front and side, drop the lead, and partly turn to face your dog and offer your right hand palm up as a wait signal and give the command Wait.

Keeping your dog on the spot with as many Sit and Wait commands as you feel necessary, continue your left hand circle at the slow pace. Then return to your dog at a slightly wider circumference. As in the Stand position, continue past for two or three revolutions before collecting your dog on the command Heel coupled with plenty of praise. Finish after a few more yards of slow straight heelwork, before breaking into normal pace prior to the halt. Don't worry about the short hanging lead still attached to your dog as this won't hinder him in the slightest.

The next step, maintaining the slow pace, is to make the first halt where you check back on the short lead with the command Sit and then step to the right, all in the same movement. Three or four repetitions of this over the course of a few days will ensure a positive and confident sit.

Completing the exercise at normal pace is a simple procedure. Build up your pace gradually thus speeding up the sits accordingly. Practice this until the short lead can be dispensed with and straight heelwork at normal pace is achieved with just the Sit command remaining. You will find that a slight body hesitation at the moment of asking your dog to sit will be beneficial and quite usual in the early stages once moving into normal pace heelwork. Very soon this hesitation will no longer be necessary as your dog understands more about what you are asking of him. As in all stages of training there is no rush. Perfection is the aim and that is seldom gained by too much haste.

The Down Position

Allow the lead to drop down to form a loop alongside your dog.

Ensure that he is watching you when you place your left foot in the loop of the lead.

If applied correctly your dog will now be flat to the ground.

I start the down position on the lead and on the spot. For a dog that has already been taught the down this comes easily, especially as the forward motion in heelwork assists the downing motion. All we need now is to introduce speed in the down to make things complete.

I use a very common method of speeding up an instant down by using my left foot in the trough of a dangling lead.

With your dog at your left side and on a normal length lead in the Attention head position, allow the lead to drop down to form a loop alongside you dog. You must ensure that the loop is positioned so that when you put your foot gently on the lead the pressure is enough to encourage your dog to go to the ground. Failure to do this will just prolong the procedure and offer your dog the option of wriggling out of the situation and become hesitant at further attempts. Like all new exercises think carefully beforehand and really consider what you are about to do so that you carry it out effectively and you make it easy for the dog to understand. At no stage must your dog think that you are making an all out attack on him.

To start with then, hold the lead in the right hand, dangle it by the dog side to form a loop and just use the Down command in your usual fashion. Just like the sit, your dog will have already learnt the Instant Down and will be happy to oblige. Reward with a titbit if using them

The next step is then to apply the pressure to the dangling lead. Do this by having the dog by your side with the loop already formed in the lead. Ensure your dog is watching you and place your left foot in the loop of the lead. Your foot and the 'stirrup' formed by the lead should be about 15 cm off the ground. That is enough for the following action to register with your dog but not to yank his head to alarm or confuse him. At the same time hold the lead tightly in your right hand and give the Down command and stamp your left foot down firmly till reaching the ground. If applied correctly your dog will now be flat to the ground in his normal Instant Down position and held in place.

The earlier Down/Stay training you did where you held the dog down by the lead while kneeling by his side will hold you in good stead here. This is because he already acquainted with the position and will not have any fears we could have created by forcing the issue. Obviously stroke your dog reassuringly with added words of praise.

Practice this on the spot on and off for some days until the movement has become second nature to the dog. You will find that if you continue with the foot movement only, without stepping on the lead, the dog will maintain his speed in dropping.

When putting the whole thing into practice attempt your first efforts in a left-handed circle. But this time go straight at normal pace and off the lead. It is important that the Instant Down is instant, and not encouraged to be slowed by working in a gentler fashion.

When comfortable with what you are doing in your left-hand circle, focus on what you are about to attempt. When the time is right, hesitate for a slight moment as you give the Down command coupled with the leg and foot downward signal. Unless you have not perfected this on the spot, or have upset your dog in some way, he will complete this manoeuvre without a second thought. It is then only a matter of time before you can drop off the leg and foot signal altogether in preparation for your ring work.

Chapter 13

Stays
The Sit, Stand and Down

Taking all other training into consideration, I consider Stay training as the most important of all as an error made here can lead to years of heartbreak and regret for the handler and misery and fear for the dog. I have absolutely no doubt that a confident, bold and temperamentally sound dog in the stay ring is a dog that carries that aura throughout the rest of his Obedience work.

I have experienced problems myself, not of my own making I will hasten to add. Many dogs that do have stay problems have had them created by outside influences or a handler who was inconsiderate to his dog's feelings by attempting far longer stays than his dog was ready for.

Like much of my training I begin my stay training in a quiet location and I always start with the Sit followed by the Stand and then finally the Down. Rather like my early Distant Control training I capitalise on my dog's moments of naturally sitting, standing and lying down by allowing them to stay in those positions while throwing in a sit/stand/flat command and giving them a tit bit combined with gentle stroking.

It is so easy to do and takes very little effort. If your dog lives in the house then just observe what he is doing. Before long he will carry out one of the actions and before the serious stuff really starts just play along with him. One of the most obvious is when a dog walks up and sits by you when you are in an armchair. Always have titbits about your person when planning something like this and when the dog sits, just say Sit and give him a titbit. But don't then give him a reward if he decides to lay down immediately afterwards, just ignore it. It was the sit you were after, nothing else.

Another good opportunity is when your dog is lying on his side. Use the Flat command as against the Down command. Leave the Down for an instant down in Sendaway or in Advanced Heelwork for the down position on the move.

Use the 'Flat' command opposed to the 'Down' command.

When your dog is just lying on his side kneel down alongside him, say Flat and give him a titbit. If he begins to move just console him quietly and coax him into staying flat if you can. If you can't, don't worry and let him get up. The important thing is that you gave him his reward while he was flat.

By doing this for some weeks, as in the pre-Distant Control stage, you are 'softening up' your dog for what is to come which is much more serious training.

My own 'hard luck' story took place at a show in Hampshire many years ago when my Merlin had only just qualified to work Class B. As he was such a good dog this came very early in his life and set the seal until he prematurely retired because of his health.

It was pouring with rain on the day and we were in the stay ring after completing the Stand Stay. The Down Stay was next so I got Merlin into his flat stay position. I was wearing yellow waterproofs rather like a lifeboat coxswain and at 'last command' I waddled off and got out of sight behind a marquee. No sooner had I done this than the Chief Stay Steward walked by the ringside and off into the crowd seeking out competitors for the next set of stays. And what was he wearing? Yes, the same yellow waterproofs as me!

Merlin raised his head to watch 'me' out of one eye but stayed on the spot. When the steward was about 100 metres away he saw the person he was looking for and waved an arm to attract his attention. Merlin was up like a shot and doing an 'A' recall. He reached the steward at breakneck speed and went into his left side like he was working in the ring.

The steward told me later that the look on Merlin's face was something to see but what worried me most was the way he reacted and ran off into the crowd in a panic. It took about 10 minutes to get him back. What must have gone through his mind during this moment of great trauma? I wondered?

Well I didn't have to wait long to find out as he became a regular stay-breaker after this incident and seemed to break every other stay.

The Sit Stay

With your dog on a lead, place him in a normal sit by your left side. On the command Sit and Stay hold the lead in your left hand about 15 cms above your dog's head. Step out to the right on your right leg before joining your left leg to meet it. Although you have moved to the right one pace your left hand must stay in the same position above the dog's head holding the lead. This is the pivotal point and it must remain so.

With your dog on a lead place him in a normal sit by your left side

By doing this you can hold the end of the lead in your right hand between the thumb and forefinger while holding the flat of that same hand up as a signal to stay on the spot. If you keep the lead between your two hands taut, it becomes like an iron bar, thus keeping your dog securely on the spot.

Now, keeping your left hand just above your dog's head move slowly anti-clockwise around the dog continually using the command Sit and Stay and holding up the flat of the right hand to face the dog even when behind him. If your dog tries to stand up slight backward/downward pressure on the lead will correct this until he is settled again. On completion of one revolution return to your dog's side and before finishing give the command Sit again and offer him a titbit.

If you keep the lead between your two hands taut it becomes like an iron bar. This keeps your dog securely on the spot.

You have completed your first Sit Stay and can release the dog and give loads of praise to finish.

Just repeat the exercise two or three more times before moving on to something completely different. At no stage ever teach all the stays together, even when more experienced.

Top Tips

■ Remember! Never teach all the stays together.

Gradually as the days move on you can extend the time you keep your dog sat in this stay position and begin to remove your left hand from above his head for short periods. Don't rush this though, it is not a race.

Once confident the next stage is to release your dog off the lead and just use the Sit and Stay commands coupled with the hand signal. This would normally come readily, but do remember to still move to the side of your dog with the right leg first. Remember also that the left leg is the leading leg so make sure you do not give false signals which could make your dog break his sit position by thinking he is going into heelwork!

From here on in it is just a question of increasing the distance away from your dog as you circle until you have both mastered the move. Always return to your dog from the side in training so that there will never be confusion with the Novice Recall if you returned from the front.

The Stand Stay

First place your dog in the Stand position like in the Distant Control exercise. I like to do this in as friendlier a way as possible as this is the position that dogs are most wary of each other. It is, afterall, the position a dog will take up when entering into an attack with another dog and personally I approve of the Kennel Club abolishing it during 2003. However, as an exercise to train stability into a dog, I am still in favour of teaching it.

Stand next to your dog on the left side with your leg underneath him.

I stand next to the dog on the left-hand side and partly slide my foot underneath him so that if he tries to sit I can give him a gentle reminder to stand by touching his stomach or chest with the top front of my foot. As normal I reward with a titbit at frequent intervals.

Once again, as in the sit stay training, when your dog gets more confident and is prepared to stand more readily just walk around him at close quarters at first so that you can easily correct him with a hand or foot if he tries to move out of position or sit down. Keep repeating the Stand command as you circle the dog but at the same time begin to increase the distance and approach from different positions. If you're not foolishly attempting to do all the various stays in succession this should not be a problem. However it can easily become an issue if you attempt multiple stays in training.

The Down Stay

So that my dogs don't confuse the Down Stay with the Instant Down as in the Sendaway or in Advanced Heelwork, I teach a Flat Down and not the more usual traditional 'lion' position. This involves making the dog lay prone on one side so that only one eye is free to face distractions that may occur.

tend the distance and the time
ent 'flat'.

Until my dog understands what Flat means I train the Flat Down in an entirely different way to my other Down Stay methods so that he understands that this is going to be a stay test rather than the Sendaway or Advanced Heelwork down.

With your dog in the sit position, kneel down alongside him with your left hand holding the collar from the side facing you. Push your right arm under the dog between the front and back legs and grab hold of his left front leg toward the top. In one quick movement and while giving the command Flat, draw the held leg towards you while pushing your left hand away and downward with the hand holding the collar.

The outcome will be a dog that has gone from the sit to the flat position in an instant.

If you had followed closely the previous suggestion at the start of this chapter of 'catching him when he did something right' then, on numerous occasions, you would have given your dog a calming Flat command and a titbit when you had seen him lying on his side while at rest. If you had, now is the time that this pays off. By applying the same criteria at this point and by calmly repeating the same command and gently stroking your dog while he is in this flat position, you will soon have him confidently lying flat on command only.

Like both the Stand and the Sit exercises, gradually extend the period spent in the flat position and walk round your dog in an ever increasing outward spiral. With practice you dog will gain confidence and competence with this position.

A good guide to how well you are doing in teaching your dog the Flat stay with this method is that within a very short space of time, the moment you go to place your arm under your dog he will go into a flat position. When this happens you know you are well on your way to succeeding.

Further Stay Training

So far you will have ideally carried out your stay training in quiet location. Once confidence is high and your dog is competent in all three stages, you can venture down to the local park or join up with a friend who has a dog and practice stays with them. A note of caution however, if you do practice with a person whose dog is forever breaking his stays and is being shouted at and being chastised all the time then beat a very hasty retreat. This is the last thing you want at this stage!

Over time you will be able to subject your dog to a much greater variety of distractions such as bangs and other noises. The aim being that by the time you are ready for the ring you have produced a happy, lively and confident dog, trouble-free and distraction proof in all of his stays.

It is also a good idea to practice stays in inclement weather. I don my wet weather gear and practice in the rain on grassy surfaces as well as tarmac and concrete. I even have my dogs sitting in streams and puddles so that they experience all manner of things, but I won't go out in thunderstorms under any circumstances.

With dogs that are frightened of sounds such as thunder and gunshot it pays you to have a tape of these recorded sounds and replay them over and over in a 'safe' environment such as in your house or garden while having fun. Again our friend 'Mr Knotty, the sock' does this admirably.

Once confident and competent you can invite other dogs (and their trainers) to practice the exercises with you both.

Top Tips

Remember! In time introduce distractions – but only when your dog is ready.

Chapter 14

Distant Control

Early introduction of the Sit, Stand and Down positions

Countless times throughout your dog's life he will sit, stand and lie down quite naturally, on his own without any coaxing from you. With a pup, as with an older rescued dog, these are the times to capitalise on the situation. Take time out for a couple of weeks to observe your pup at play and at rest and with the use of titbits make full use of the situations presented to you. In fact much of the early work, as we have already seen, can be done whilst sitting in your favourite chair while both you and your dog are relaxing.

Should your dog be lying down, for instance, in the traditional 'lion' position just stroke him gently and while giving him the Down command, pop a titbit into his mouth followed by praise. If he should be sitting or standing at the time, do exactly the same but with the Sit or Stand commands. Doing this will give the chance beforehand to get used to the commands you will be using and an understanding of what will be expected of him.

Holding a titbit above the head is the easiest way to obtain a sit from the stand position.

To achieve the down from the stand take him through to the sit first then lower the titbit down to encourage your dog to follow.

The Sit Position from the Stand

The sit position from the stand is easily achieved by holding a titbit directly above your dog's head. As soon as he shows interest in the titbit move it backwards above his head. It seems very natural for him to sit to observe what is above him. Give the Sit command and reward him as soon as he does. If your dog doesn't sit straight away, allow him a little more time to work out what you are asking of him. If he then does it correctly reward him in exactly the same way. As soon as he has worked this out, sits will then become amazingly fast. If you prefer you may keep your dog on a lead for this exercise and use it to your advantage by applying slight backwards pressure until the dog sits. You may also consider backing your dog up to a wall to stop him moving backwards.

If your dog should try and jump up to meet your hand carrying the titbit, just ignore the action, retain the titbit and start over again. Very soon he will catch on and will be obeying you instantly.

The Down Position from the Stand via the Sit

The down position from the stand is again easily achieved. First carry out the stand to the sit position. Secondly, hold a titbit by your dog's mouth. As he tries to take it slowly lower your hand downwards and close to his chest then down to the ground. As your dog tries to get the titbit draw your hand slowly along the floor until he is in the down position. Give the Down command as soon as he has done it and reward with the titbit. If you prefer you may apply slight downward pressure on the lead but it probably won't be necessary as your dog will soon work out that by following your hand there is a reward on offer!

If there is a reluctance to stand slide your foot gently between your dog's front legs until it touches the lower part of his chest.

The Stand Position from the Sit

Starting in the sit position and with a titbit in your hand, stand immediately in front of your dog. Say your dog's name followed by the command you intend using, commonly Stand or Back, and walk towards your dog. Most dogs will automatically stand as you approach them. This is when you give the titbit and praise.

If there is a reluctance to stand, slide a foot gently between the dog's front legs until it touches the lower part of his chest. This normally makes the dog stand and move back slightly. Once again give your Stand command where appropriate and lavish reward and praise on completion. Another successful method is to just gently push the dog's toes with a foot as you approach him and as he withdraws them he will almost certainly stand.

Plenty of praise here with a titbit as a reward.

Down to the Stand

By this time the dog is well aware of the reward he gets for comple[ ]ing a position simply by following your hand which holds the titbit. [ ]should be an easy matter to just do the same for the Down to th[ ]Stand.

With your dog in the 'lion' down position stand about 1 metre in fro[ ]with a titbit in your right hand. Walk towards him with that har[ ]above his head while giving him the command Sit. As he tries to get th[ ]titbit raise your hand up and backwards until your dog is in the s[ ]position. Don't hurry your hand movement as you need to ensure th[ ]the dog realises that you have a reward in it and he will get it if h[ ]'plays the game.'

If your dog is reluctant to move up into the sit, then, as you move fo[ ]ward with the titbit bring your right foot forward along the ground a[ ]touch the dog's toes. This normally has the desired effect and oft[ ]makes him stand without further need to do anything else. However, [ ]it doesn't then of course it's just a matter of following through with th[ ]gentle foot under the chest to make him stand as described in the pr[ ]vious Sit to the Stand section.

Other than the possible use of a gentle foot for the stand and slight pre[ ]sure on the lead, all of the three positions can been completed witho[ ]forcing the dog to do anything other than what he wanted to do of his [ ]volition. Training of this type is a joy and just goes to show what can [ ]achieved when reward training is carried out patiently and deliberate[ ]

After many days and even weeks of 'fun' Distant Control training on the spot, the time comes when your dog must be prepared for his ring work. As its name suggests, this is attempted at a distance from the handler so confidence in this set piece exercise is of vital importance. As the Kennel Club regulations state, there are six positions to perform in the ring. They can be in any order, but as an example and from being left in a sit position, they may be like this:

1. Sit to a Down.

2. Down to a Stand.

3. Stand to a Sit.

4. Sit to a Stand.

5. Stand to a Down

6. Down to a Sit.

As you can see, each set position i.e. Sit, Stand or Down, must be followed by one of the other two until all the combinations are completed.

To prepare my dog for Distant Control in the ring I construct a training box for carrying out the basics before I progress any further.

simple training box can be made
initial training of the Distant
ntrol (shown here without the
k panel).

With your dog in the training box carry out all the initial training until it is performed with confidence and the box is fully accepted.

But firstly, the training box.

For the base I use a piece of plywood or similar 1 metre long by 25cm wide. To the front of the box I fix an upright board 15cms high and t the sides a 10 cm high board. I have no back board as initially encourage backward movement. The box allows the dog the room t carry out all the positions required without making forward groun and restricting sideways movement to within acceptable limits.

Although my box is portable there is no reason why you can't make in a set position in your garden with just the sides, front and no base The sides and front don't even need to be secured to one and other a long as they are secured in place with ground pegs or similar.

For a day or two allow your dog to get used to the box by placing hi feed bowl in it at feeding time. Like all our training thus far, food an titbits have been a calming and rewarding influence whenever wor has been asked for and carried out. Your dog will learn to recognis this aspect of training and will soon willingly walk into the box withou fear or apprehension.

With your dog in the training box, carry out all the initial training a previously described until it is performed with confidence and verv and the box is fully accepted. Insure that when you commence you training in the box your dog's paws are up to the front barrier. Yc will find that your dog will soon adjust to the box's sides and front ba rier, and other than backward movement will take it all in his stride.

You will also find by this time that the hand movement with the titb can be gradually dropped off and the reward only given when the actio has been carried out. A simple Stand, Sit, Down command with th pretence of a hand signal will then suffice until you are able to ju rely on your voice commands.

A word of warning about the voice commands. While it is, of course, sensible to use the dog's name before the command when first teaching the dog to gain attention, be aware that many dogs will begin to anticipate the moves in the ring. They see their name as a precursor to a position and will often choose what they sense it is going to be by the tone in your voice. Therefore it would be wise to just use the selected command only until maybe the Down to the Stand position is required, when often you need all the help you can get!

With regard to the Down to the Stand, well, where earlier you had used your foot gently against the dog's feet for the stand, you can now only rely on the foot motion, as the barrier to the front of the box prevents the actual intervention of the foot.

Many dogs by this time will simply stand if you 'ghost' the foot movement in front of them, but for those that do not I then introduce a sliding inner front barrier to the box.

I cut a length of board the same height as the existing front board but short enough to fit inside the width of the box with ease. I attach this short board to a 1 metre length of 3 cm round pole or a shortened broom handle shaft and drill a suitable size hole though the fixed front board to accommodate it. Alternatively have the front panel raised allowing sufficient room for the pole/broom handle to slide underneath it. The board facing the dog can be padded if your prefer.

It is then a simple matter of just standing that 1 metre in front of the training box and as you give the Stand command, move your foot forward as usual. This time though, apply a little backward pressure on the broom handle that will cause the inner barrier to slide back and touch the dog's toes and encourage him to carry out the desired action on the chosen command.

In time you can gradually move further back and by still using the forward foot movement as a signal, accomplish a perfect Stand from the down while the training box ensures the dog stays in the perfect position throughout.

Remember though, throughout all of this, keep tit-bits handy and give them as a form of reward whenever you feel your dog has carried out what has been asked of him perfectly. An imperfect position gains no reward and this will soon be recognised and understood by any normally responsive dog.

Once the training box has served its purpose it can be removed and simple piece of wood about two feet wide and about 5 cms square placed on the ground will do ideally as a frontal barrier to assist complete the training with.

Run through all the positions again until confident, then, replace the new barrier with a 5 cm wide strip of tape or similar secured to the ground until finally all aids can be dispensed with as you are left with the finished article ready to do you proud in the ring.

Chapter 15

Summary

So the moment has come. You have taken your time and haven't hurried. Everything has fallen into place. Your basic training has been done in a methodical and practical manner. The proof of the pudding is now in the eating!

You and your dog are now ready to enter the ring in your first show

So where do you start and what are the golden rules to observe when competing?

Not too long ago Exemption Dog Shows were very popular but, alas, they are a lot rarer now. These are shows that, although held under KC license, were designed to be not taken too seriously and were a gentle way of introducing the newcomer into competitive Obedience without putting too much pressure on them. Trophies and rosettes are handed out but winning did not qualify you out of any Open Show classes. They are still about and if you see one advertised then go along on the day and enter the classes you feel your level of 'experience' can handle. They can be a great source of fun and a wonderful opportunity for you and your dog to sample working under show conditions.

As a newcomer to the sport, things are obviously going to feel rather strange at first. It may be that you have been fortunate enough to have trained in the company of a friend. If this is the case, then it would be beneficial for you both to enter the same show to give each other the confidence and support often needed at this very exciting, but nevertheless, nervous time.

Now all Exemption Shows are entered on the day of the show, but with Open Shows it is different. They have closing dates, normally about one month prior to them taking place, so make sure you find out about them way in advance. Dog Training Weekly and Obedience Info magazines are good sources as is the Kennel Club Gazette for major shows.

If you and your dog have never competed before then you will be eligible to work in the Pre-Beginner class at an Open show. The Kennel Club rules also allow you to work one other higher class of your choice as long as you have entered your lowest eligible class. It has to be your decision of course whether you do this or not, but most competitors generally also enter the next class up, which on this occasion would be Beginners.

Prior to walking into the ring to compete, take on a professional attitude. Most newcomers are very nervous and hesitant and take this with them into the ring. It travels down the lead and influences your dog. The result is normally a handler, who, because of tension, misses out commands, sends their dogs wrong and generally has a miserable time.

Rise above all of this and don't rush into the ring. Give a great deal of thought to what you are about to do and in particular, to your dog. He is not able to do this, so do his thinking for him, always!

In my very first show with Boots I was terrified. I had trained him very well, so I had been told, but that meant nothing to me at that moment. My instructor had previously taken me to one side and graciously imparted his vast experience to me on preparation, but for few minutes I was numbed at the thought of entering the ring and my legs were like jelly. However I put into practice what I had been taught. Luckily I had no running order so was free to work whenever I chose within reason, to be fair on the judge and not to keep him waiting. I was also equally lucky for I had a judge, the late Don Gardner, who was renowned for his understanding and helpful way with beginner handlers. Don was a real gentleman and it was a privilege to compete under him at my first show. As my trainer had advised me to do I sat and watched countless dogs and handlers coming in and out of the ring and observed their style of work. I memorised every turn and sit, every move the judge and caller steward made until I could then go to a quiet area of the show ground and practice. By the time I entered the ring to work I already had a huge advantage and Boots sailed around the ring only losing 1.5 marks. After our stays had been completed successfully Don awarded us first place. The advice I was given was correct and I have adopted the same approach ever since. I never go into the ring' cold' and I observe every little aspect beforehand so that if errors are to be made, then it is by something out of my control.

It is also interesting to note how others approach entering the ring. Paula Wright, who has been competing successfully in Obedience for short while and who was kind enough to take the majority of the photographs in this book, has learnt well, and offers this advice which I totally agree with.

1) Smile! No matter how nervous you are as you enter the ring, make an effort to smile and be happy towards the judge and steward. You may be smiling AT them, but you are smiling for YOURSELF and YOUR dog. It will make a difference to your dog if he thinks you are happy and enjoying yourself.

2) Show off! Whatever else is going on in and around the show, just remember, you have a loyal and faithful friend by your side, even if you both sometimes get in a muddle. You always take the best dog home with you at the end of every show so be proud to "Show him off"

3) However, if you feel that things are going wrong, then just do the best you can and carry on. It is never the end of the world, and, after all, it isn't a crime to mess up.

4) Don't take what you may perceive as bad advice from judges to heart. If they offer advice listen politely, thank them, smile and then go back to your regular trainer and discuss any points that arose. You and your trainer know your dog well where the judge has only seen you and your dog for just a few anxious minutes.

5) Never argue with a judge (it is against the rules to question the judge's decision anyway) If you disagree with them just keep it to yourself, thank them and leave the ring on completion of your work. Like you, they are only doing the best job they can and sometimes we all get things wrong. It's only a hobby and there will always be another day.

6) If you need to know anything ASK! The show secretary or manager are always available and are there to help. But remember, everyone in the show ground who competes was a beginner at one time and other competitors are usually only too pleased to help.

You and your dog have come a long way since opening the first page of this book. If you have followed my advice and taken your time and treated every exercise in the correct manner you are going to be successful.

Have fun and enjoy.